I0030094

Gilles Paquet and Tim Ragan

Through the Detox Prism

Exploring Organizational Failures
and Design Responses

| Collaborative Decentred Metagovernance Series

This series of books is designed to define cumulatively the contours of collaborative decentred metagovernance. At this time, there is still no canonical version of this paradigm: it is *en émergence*. This series intends to be one of many construction sites to experiment with various dimensions of an effective and practical version of this new approach.

Metagovernance is the art of combining different forms or styles of governance – experimented within the private, public and solidarity sectors – to ensure effective coordination when power, resources and information are widely distributed, and the governing is, of necessity, decentred and collaborative.

The series invites conceptual and practical contributions focused on different issues domains, policy fields, *causes célèbres*, functional processes, etc. to the extent that they contribute to sharpening the new apparatus associated with collaborative decentred metagovernance.

In the last few decades, there has been a need felt for a more sophisticated understanding of the governing of the private, public and social sectors, for less compartmentalization among sectors that have much in common, and for new conceptual tools to suggest new relevant questions and new ways to carry the business of governing by creatively recombining the tools of governance that have proved successful in all these sectors. These efforts have generated experiments that have been sufficiently rich and wide-ranging in the various laboratories to warrant efforts to pull together what we know at this stage.

This third volume in the series deals with the collaborative decentred metagovernance challenge at the meso-organizational level. It identifies some of the most potentially toxic interfaces within organizations and, in relation to their context, seeks to extricate the sources and causes of the toxicities and coordination failures at these interfaces, and proposes ways in which organizational redesign might help to mitigate and eliminate the harms generated by these pathologies.

Interested parties are invited to join the Chautauqua.

– Editorial Board

Other titles published by INVENIRE are listed at the end of this book.

Gilles Paquet and Tim Ragan

Through the Detox Prism

Exploring Organizational Failures
and Design Responses

Collaborative Decentred Metagovernance Series

INVENIRE BOOKS

Ottawa, Canada

2012

University of Ottawa **Press**
Les **Presses** de l'Université d'Ottawa

The University of Ottawa Press (UOP) is proud to be the oldest of the francophone university presses in Canada and the oldest bilingual university publisher in North America. Since 1936, UOP has been enriching intellectual and cultural discourse by producing peer-reviewed and award-winning books in the humanities and social sciences, in French and in English.

www.Press.uOttawa.ca

Library and Archives Canada Cataloguing in Publication

Title: Through the detox prism : exploring organizational failures and design responses / Gilles Paquet and Tim Ragan.
Names: Paquet, Gilles. author. | Ragan, Tim, 1960- author.
Series: Collaborative decentred metagovernance series ; v. 3.
Description: Series statement: Collaborative decentred metagovernance series ; 3 | Reprint. Originally published: Ottawa, ON : Invenire Books, 2012. | Includes bibliographical references.
Identifiers: Canadiana (print) 20220285489 | Canadiana (ebook) 20220285543 | ISBN 9780776638829 (softcover) | ISBN 9780776638836 (PDF) | ISBN 9780776638843 (EPUB)
Subjects: LCSH: Organizational change. | LCSH: Organizational effectiveness. | LCSH: Corporate governance. | LCSH: Public administration. | LCSH: Industrial management.
Classification: LCC HD58.8 .P36 2022 | DDC 658.4/02—dc23

Legal Deposit: Library and Archives Canada, Third Quarter 2022
© University of Ottawa Press 2022, all rights reserved.

This book was initially published by Invenire Books in 2012 in the Collaborative Decentered Metagovernance Series. The cover design, layout and design were produced by Sandy Lynch. The University of Ottawa Press reissued this book thanks to the support of Ontario Creates.

Invenire

Invenire Books, an Ottawa-based idea factory that operated from 2010 to 2019, specialized in collaborative governance and stewardship. Invenire and its authors provide creative practical and stimulating responses to the challenges and opportunities faced by today's organizations. The list is now carried by the University of Ottawa Press.

Profession: Public Servant
The Entrepreneurial Effect: Practical Ideas from Your Own Virtual Board of Advisors
La flotte blanche : histoire de la compagnie de navigation du Richelieu et d'Ontario
Tableau d'avancement II : essais exploratoires sur la gouvernance d'un certain Canada français
The Entrepreneurial Effect: Waterloo
The Unimagined Canadian Capital: Challenges for the Federal Capital Region
The State in Transition: Challenges for Canadian Federalism
Cities as Crucibles: Reflections on Canada's Urban Future
Gouvernance communautaire : innovations dans le Canada français hors Québec
Through the Detox Prism: Exploring Organizational Failures and Design Responses
Cities and Languages: Governance and Policy – An International Symposium
Villes et langues : gouvernance et politiques – symposium international
Moderato Cantabile: Toward Principled Governance for Canada's Immigration Policy
Stewardship: Collaborative Decentred Metagovernance and Inquiring Systems
Challenges in Public Health Governance: The Canadian Experience
Innovation in Canada: Why We Need More and What We Must Do to Get It
Challenges of Minority Governments in Canada
Gouvernance corporative : une entrée en matières

Tackling Wicked Policy Problems: Equality, Diversity and Sustainability
50 ans de bilinguisme officiel : défis, analyses et témoignages
Unusual Suspects: Essays on Social Learning
Probing the Bureaucratic Mind: About Canadian Federal Executives
Tableau d'avancement III : pour une diaspora canadienne-française antifragile
Autour de Chantal Mouffe : le politique en conflit
Town and Crown: An Illustrated History of Canada's Capital
The Tainted-Blood Tragedy in Canada: A Cascade of Governance Failures
Intelligent Governance: A Prototype for Social Coordination
Driving the Fake Out of Public Administration: Detoxing HR in the Canadian Federal Public Sector
Tableau d'avancement IV : un Canada français à ré-inventer
A Future for Economics: More Encompassing, More Institutional, More Practical
Pasquinade en F : essais à rebrousse-poil
Building Bridges: Case Studies in Collaborative Governance in Canada
Scheming Virtuously: The Road to Collaborative Governance
A Lantern on the Bow: A History of the Science Council of Canada and its Contributions to the Science and Innovation Policy Debate
Fifty Years of Official Bilingualism: Challenges, Analyses and Testimonies
Irregular Governance: A Plea for Bold Organizational Experimentation
Pasquinade in E: Slaughtering Some Sacred Cows

The University of Ottawa Press gratefully acknowledges the support extended to its publishing list by the Government of Canada, the Canada Council for the Arts, the Ontario Arts Council, the Social Sciences and Humanities Research Council and the Canadian Federation for the Humanities and Social Sciences through the Awards to Scholarly Publications Program, and by the University of Ottawa.

ONTARIO ARTS COUNCIL
CONSEIL DES ARTS DE L'ONTARIO
an Ontario government agency
un organisme du gouvernement de l'Ontario

Canada Council   Conseil des arts
for the Arts   du Canada

Canadä

uOttawa

Scrutinizing the harms themselves, and discovering their dynamics and dependencies, leads to the possibility of sabotage. Cleverly conceived acts of sabotage, exploiting identified vulnerabilities of the object under attack, can be not only effective, but extremely resource-efficient too.

– *Malcolm Sparrow*

It is impossible to wake someone who is only pretending to sleep.

– *Traditional Somali saying*

| Table of Contents

INTRODUCTION
| About detoxification as a new way of thinking

This short book is the joint work of an organizational economist and a business engineer. It stems from their joint conviction that many of the important problems of the day in the meso-organizations of modern socio-economies cannot be effectively dealt with because of two major biases in the way most social scientists conduct their work.

The first bias is the propensity for analysts to focus either on broad general macro-phenomena like growth, development, progress or the like, or on the minutiae of single incidents or cases studies – in the language of the sociologists: urbanization in the Western world or street-corner societies. This is the case, even though much that is of practical import would rather call for an approach *at the meso-level*, in the messy middle ground of the interfaces among groups where issues and problems crystallize. This is an approach sufficiently focused to allow a full grasp of local circumstances, but sufficiently broad to take into account the networks and mega-communities within which the organization is nested.[1]

The second bias is the rather optimistic 'Rousseauist' flavour of most social scientists (even though to a lesser degree in the dismal science of economics) that leads practitioners to focus their attention on good things like efficiency, happiness and the

[1] Mark Gerencser et al. 2008. *Megacommunities*. New York: Palgrave Macmillan.

THROUGH THE DETOX PRISM

like, and spend much less time on countervailing bad things, on scrutinizing harms, systemic failures or dysfunctions and the like. A more 'Voltairian' attitude – that things are usually failing – would suggest that there is much merit in giving some priority to dealing with harms.

Others have adopted a meso-approach and focused on pathologies and harms. The works of Corrado Gini, Albert Hirschman, Elinor Ostrom, Thomas Schelling, Malcolm Sparrow and Oliver Williamson among others come to mind.[2] However, their work has been in general much more ambitious than ours: they aimed at little less than a general theory of socio-economic pathology.

Our purpose is immensely more modest. We wish to explore only a few toxic features of meso-organizations that may throw some light on our modern-day dysfunctions that are crippling productivity, resilience, innovation, safety and survival (processes that are at the foundation not only of organizational success, but also of our standard of living and of a good life), to probe the proximate sources of these pathologies, and to suggest how some redesign work might help to overcome or attenuate these dysfunctions at least in part.

A meso-approach focusing on pathologies

This project was born of the experience of some critical and reconstructive work of the two authors in the public/social and private sectors respectively.[3] This work revealed that a pattern of pathologies could be observed in the governance of private, public and social concerns. These pathologies

[2] Corrado Gini. 1959. *Pathologie économique*. Paris: Payot; Albert O. Hirschman. 1970. *Exit, Voice and Loyalty – Responses to Decline in Firms, Organizations and States*. Cambridge, MA: Harvard University Press; Elinor Ostrom. 2005. *Understanding Institutional Diversity*. Princeton: Princeton University Press; Thomas C. Schelling. 1973. *Micromotives and Macrobehavior*. New York: Norton; Malcolm K. Sparrow. 2008. *The Character of Harms*. Cambridge, UK: Cambridge University Press; Oliver E. Williamson. 1995. *The Mechanisms of Governance*. New York: Oxford University Press.

[3] Gilles Paquet. 2009. *Crippling Epistemologies and Governance Failures – A Plea for Experimentalism*. Ottawa: University of Ottawa Press; Tim Ragan. 2010. "The Detox Project," www.optimumonline.ca, 40(3): 53-58.

would appear to emerge from coordination failures at certain key junctions or interfaces within organizations, or between organizations and their environment in space and time. *The Detox Prism* presents a novel way of exploring these interfaces and identifying how they manifest many of the toxic outcomes of modern institutions.

Too often, such coordination failures are ascribed to particular actors or groups (labour unions, lobbyists, CEOs, selected shareholders, etc.) or to their greed, when in fact they are most often the unintended consequences of faulty, incomplete or ill-suited organization design (and associated rules and behaviours). Such faulty design is often the source (1) of the pathological dynamics of interactions among actors whose behaviour is based on myopic or reductive or information-deficient perspectives, and on more or less rational reactions to the provocations of other agents; and (2) of the poor appreciation of the forces of self-organization that prevents the organization design from meeting effectively the daunting challenges of the Other, the Uncertain, the New and the Transcendent.[4]

Some of the important work of Elinor Ostrom (co-winner of the Nobel Prize in Economics in 2009) has shown that individuals and groups can develop an appreciation of these predicaments. She has provided empirical evidence that they can collaboratively develop design capacities, and construct mechanisms and contraptions to overcome these limitations, and thereby repair all sorts of tragedy-of-the-commons-type and other types of coordination failures. Such design work can ensure not only efficiency, but also justice and morality.[5]

To gain an appreciation of the dynamics of the toxic pathologies at work requires a good understanding of the context, of the texture of particular families of organizations, and of the dynamics of the process of stewardship of organizations

---

[4] Gilles Paquet. 2011a. *Tableau d'avancement II – Essais exploratoires sur un certain Canada français.* Ottawa: Invenire, part IV; Gilles Paquet. 2011b. *Gouvernance collaborative: un antimanuel.* Montreal: Liber, chapters 3-4.

[5] Elinor Ostrom et al. 1992. "Covenants with and without a sword: self-governance is possible," *The American Political Science Review,* 86(2): 404-417; Stan van Hooft. 2006. *Virtue Ethics.* Chesham: Acumen, chapter 4.

based in part on design and in part on self-organization – all
this always evolving as circumstances change and as guiding
beliefs, principles, and norms also get transformed.[6]

At the very core of such work is the notion of *stewardship as
inquiring systems* mobilizing and motivating key stakeholders
(1) who have a portion of the information, power and resources;
(2) who are capable of generating the requisite wayfinding
through collaborative social learning; and, (3) who can assure
the continuing invention of new ways to ensure the resilience
and survival (in ever renewed forms) of the organization.

Stewardship is embodied in a variety of mechanisms
making up something like an active feedback learning loop,
such as an automatic pilot feature on an airplane – if we are
allowed to use this metaphor – that (1) monitors the changes
in the environment, the functioning of the organization, and
the surprise and novelty generated by the context and the
interactions among all individuals and groups; and, (2) reacts
creatively to the tensions experienced. To do so, sensitivity to
each problematic area and to its revealing gaps between the
observed and the desirable fit with the environment, leads to
corrective action geared to ensure the required innovations to
cope with contextual and interactional challenges. This is at the
core of the learning journeys.[7]

There are a number of "sensors" that need monitoring in
order to gain a good appreciation of the organization, to
generate a meaningful diagnosis of the problems experienced,
and to enable the design of the pattern of interventions required.
Yet there are a few key interfaces and their related sensors
that would appear to be relatively more important than the
others as the loci of potentially important design flaws where
redesign efforts might get the most "bang for the buck."

---

[6] Ruth Hubbard, Gilles Paquet and Christopher Wilson. 2012. *Stewardship –
Collaborative Decentred Metagovernance and Inquiring Systems*. Ottawa: Invenire.

[7] Peter Senge 1990. *The Fifth Discipline – The art and practice of the learning
organization*. New York: Doubleday; Peter Senge et al. 2008. *The Necessary
Revolution – how individuals and organizations are working together to create a
sustainable world*. New York: Doubleday.

The Detox Prism: a five-dimensional framework
The Detox Prism identifes five main clusters of coordination failures at these key interfaces:
- the interface between the organization and its employees;
- the interface between the organization and its matrix of other partners in the production process of products or services;
- the interface between the organization and its socio-physical environment;
- the interface between the array of key stakeholders involved and the governance regime intended to provide good stewardship; and,
- the interface between the organization and the cultural, moral and ethical context within which it is nested.[8]

Corresponding to each of these interfaces, we have identified some crucial problems at the source of the dysfunctions:
- "X-inefficiencies" – generated by shirking and wasteful lack of coordination in the labour process;
- "escaping fault" – as a result of complexity, slack and irresponsibility in the value-adding chain/matrix;
- "externalities" – at the source of the gap between private and social decision-making and sets of accounts;
- "hijacking" – at the origin of the hegemony of certain groups on the misguided stewardship of the organization; and,
- "moral vacancy" – at the root of the 'unboundedness' of the behaviour of actors and partners leading to excesses.

Obviously these five key interfaces are inter-related to the extent that failure of coordination at one or the other interfaces is generally ascribable to some failure of trust, and that distrust at one interface spreads readily to others. As can be seen in

[8] This fifth dimension might appear a bit exotic. This is not the case. There are good reasons to believe that morality (like language, rationality and culture) is a trait that sets humans apart from their primate relatives. Therefore the ultra-sociality constraints, generated in the realm of the spiritual, the transcendent, and the moral, have an impact on the foundation of the social order. (Charles Taylor. 2007. *A Secular Age*. Cambridge, MA: Harvard University Press; Joseph Heath. 2008. *Following the Rules*. Oxford, UK: Oxford University Press; Gilles Paquet, 2011a, chapter III).

Figure 1, this gives moral vacancy a central importance in this complex of relationships: it may be surmised that the occurrence of distrust at the different nodes is in good part ascribable to some degree of moral vacancy, and that distrust at the other four interfaces feed the general moral vacancy.

While these five interfaces are not the only ones of significance, they are of general interest in most meso-organizations. The focus of this work will therefore be (1) to define the nature of the families of pathologies detected at these interfaces; (2) to determine the sources of these toxicities; (3) to suggest ways in which coordination failures can be repaired and harms attenuated by some redesign; and, (4) to illustrate how it might work in the real world by providing a sketchy presentation of either some instances where such redesign work appears to have worked well, or at least some general guidance as to useful directions for repair work.

In the next chapters, we use this four-step approach to probe the toxic problems raised at these five interfaces. We would surmise that these problems may be the sources of something like two-thirds to three-quarters of the dysfunctions of meso-organizations – a rough indication of the central importance of the challenge of redesign at these frontiers.[9]

---

[9] Even though this order of magnitude is at best a 'guesstimate,' we shall see throughout the book that it is not a fanciful one.

FIGURE 1: Key sources of the dysfunctions

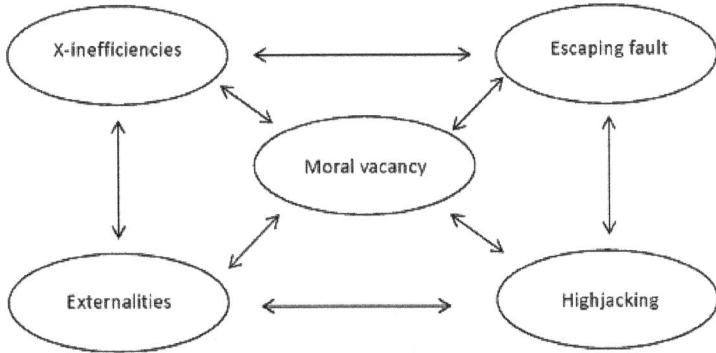

X-inefficiencies

Escaping fault

Moral vacancy

Externalities

Highjacking

Contribution to collaborative decentred metagovernance
This book is published in the Collaborative Decentred Metagovernance Series that focuses on the art of combining different forms or styles of governing (experimented within the private, public and social sectors) to ensure collaborative and decentred coordination when power, resources and information are widely distributed. It builds on the premise that, in the face of organizational failures, the various stakeholders need to be coaxed into participating actively in the inquiring process of co-governing to generate the repair work that is required in meso-organizations giving signs of stress, and that their stewardship work will be constrained by the power of context and self-organization.

Without trying to anticipate the lessons learned from this journey, a provisional look at some general results of the sort of work we are engaged in might give the reader a sense of direction as he/she enters the book.

First, our earlier work suggests that the five selected interfaces of the Detox Prism are some of the most important loci of coordination friction or failures at the core of the collaborative decentred governance of organizations, and that the design repairs at these interfaces cannot be done exclusively with market mechanisms or hierarchical controls.

Voluntary self-enforcing conventions or moral contracts[10] (based on mutual recognition and organizational culture, but also on norms and principles) are crucial for collaboration to work.[11]

Second, the toxicities that have developed at these interfaces are responsible not only for pathologies of governance at this particular locus but also for significant distortions in the ethos that emerge as a matter of consequence of these local pathologies, as they reverberate throughout all aspects of the operations of the overall organization. As a result of these important indirect effects on efficiency, commitment and quality of effort and the like, in general, there is a weakening of the organizational culture, and some echo effects of these dysfunctions on the moral order underpinning it.[12] As a result, design flaws observed at one interface may have detrimental second and third-order effects on the other interfaces, on the ethos of the organization, and contribute in a significant way to the erosion of the moral order.

---

[10] Gilles Paquet. 1999. "Betting on Moral Contracts" in *Governance through Social Learning* by G. Paquet. Ottawa: University of Ottawa Press, chapter 12.

[11] There has been an unhealthy suspicion in the private sector, in particular, of moral contracts and self-enforcing arrangements based on trust. This has led to an absurd dismissal of one family of ways of getting things done (Gerard Fairtlough. 2005. *The Three Ways of Getting Things Done: Hierarchy, Heterarchy and Responsible Autonomy in Organization.* Dorset: Triarchy Press). The third way has already proved quite successful, as in the case of Caterpillar – the grand old firm of heavy equipment – being transformed into 3,000 communities of practice, a firm, of which 70 percent of the assets were heavy equipment, has become one where 85 percent of the assets are intellectual capital entirely based on communities of practice, trust and voluntary self-enforcing conventions (Vicki Powers. 2004. "Virtual Communities at Caterpillar Foster Knowledge Sharing," *Training & Development* (June)). It has also been shown that effective regulation does not necessarily proceed in an adversarial mode but as creative interplay between state regulation and self-regulation by industry (Ian Ayres and John Braithwaite. 1992. *Responsive Regulation: Transcending the Deregulation Debate.* New York: Oxford University Press).

[12] Harvey Leibenstein. 1987. *Inside the Firm.* Cambridge, MA: Harvard University Press.

Third, as Donald Schön has argued, organizations and meso-social systems contain structure, theory and technology: a set of roles and relations, views held within the organization or system about its purposes, operations, underpinning principles and future, and the prevailing technology in the operations of the system. These three dimensions are interdependent and one cannot change one without inducing change in the others.[13] While it would appear to be easier to modify the technology than the structure, and the structure than the theory, no significant redesign work can leave any dimension untouched. Moreover, the optimal sequence in particular circumstances may not be what might appear to be the easiest and most convenient.

Fourth, the stewardship of organizations and social systems depends very much on a high degree of friction, inertia and self-organization that may constrain or reinforce the dynamics of the system and/or the effectiveness of the redesign process. This increases the degree of complexity of the task at hand, and therefore the complexity of the design work – in line with Ashby's law of requisite variety which states that, for effective regulation, the variety of the regulator must be equal to or greater than the variety of the system being regulated.[14] The complexity of redesign efforts must match the degree of complexity of the system, and cannot ignore the powerful forces of self-organization.

Finally, the fact that relevant knowledge and information is spread over a number of stakeholders means that it cannot be presumed to be fully in the hands of a single actor. Information may be informal, tacit or not easily tapped, and the central challenge of stewarding entails the Herculean task of mobilizing this scattered information, and of engaging those holding it to work collaboratively (by making the highest and best use of the common public culture as infrastructure) if they are to face successfully the challenges of today and tomorrow. Redesign efforts must leverage not only

[13] Donald A. Schön. 1971. *Beyond the Stable State*. New York: Norton, p. 31ff.
[14] W. Ross Ashby. 1956. *Introduction to Cybernetics*. London: Chapman & Hall.

material resources, but also social, interpersonal and moral enabling resources.[15]

It is within the general framework defined by these broad constraints that we are going to gauge the toxicity of the five interfaces, probe their sources, and suggest useful families of repairs based on a mix of various mechanisms in use in the different sectors.

The logic of our inquiry

As suggested in the introductory volume of this collection,[16] one of the key assumptions of the proposed approach is a focus on process.

Contrary to the long tradition in social sciences that considers that *"les faits sociaux sont des choses,"* and that positivism and scientism therefore apply, the process approach does not deny that things or objects exist, but it suggests that social structures are rooted in the processes that have generated them and that they are best understood through an analysis of these processes. This is why positivism and scientism have been said to be unfit for the social sciences.[17]

An offshoot of this perspective is that intervening in processes is in the nature of design and that design cannot always be simply reduced to problem-solving steps, fully programmable under a set of rules.[18] This conventional way of defining design is unduly reductive, since it assumes that the problem space (like an actual maze) has a structure that is already given.

The design process does not really start with such givens. Schön defines it as *intelligent exploration of a terrain* (Schön 1990: 125), as an inquiry guided by an appreciative system (carried over from history and past experience) that produces

---

[15] U.G. Foa. 1971. "Interpersonal and Economic Resources," *Science,* 171(3969): 345-351.

[16] Ruth Hubbard, Gilles Paquet and Christopher Wilson, 2012, chapter 1.

[17] Friedrich A. Hayek. 1952. *Scientism and the Science of Society.* Glencoe, IL: The Free Press.

[18] Donald A. Schön. 1990. "The Design Process" in *Varieties of Thinking,* V.A. Howard (ed.). New York: Routledge, p. 110-141.

"a selective representation of an unfamiliar situation that sets values for the system's transformation. It frames the problem of the problematic situation and thereby sets directions in which solutions lie and provides a schema for exploring them" (Ibid.: 131-132).

Designing is a conversation with the situation that leads to experimenting with rules and guideposts, that, in turn, reveal conflicts among partners and dilemmas in the appreciative system. Since participants talk across discrepant frames, designing "is a process in which communication, political struggle, and substantive inquiry are combined ... [and it] may be judged appropriate ... if it leads to the creation of a design structure that directs inquiry toward progressively greater inclusion of features of the problematic situation and values for its transformation" (Ibid.: 138-139).

Such exploration leads to learning by doing, and "involves inquiry into systems that do not yet exist."[19] This new way of thinking builds on experimentation, prototyping and serious play,[20] and makes the highest and best use of grappling, grasping, discerning and sense-making as part of reflective generative learning.[21]

Our inquiry in this volume proceeds in stages: from the study of processes within the organization, to linking them to the very proximate interaction order, and then to examining the interfaces with the broader environment – as it changes in time and space; we then look at the texture of stewardship

---

[19] A. George L. Romme. 2003. "Making a Difference: Organization as Design," *Organization Science*, 14(5): 558.

[20] Prototyping means (1) identifying as quickly as possible some top requirements; (2) putting in place a quick-and-dirty provisional medium of co-development; (3) allowing as many interested parties as possible to get involved as partners in designing a better arrangement; (4) encouraging iterative prototyping; and, (5) thereby encouraging all, through playing with prototypes, to get a better understanding of the problems, of their priorities and of themselves (Gilles Paquet. 2009. *Crippling Epistemologies and Governance Failures – A Plea for Experimentalism*. Ottawa: University of Ottawa Press, p. 8; Michael Schrage. 2000. *Serious Play*. Cambridge, MA: Harvard Business School Press, p. 199ff).

[21] R.P. Chait et al. 2005. *Governance as Leadership*. Hoboken, NJ: Wiley, chapter 6.

and at the way in which the social order interacts with the moral order.

In closing, we try to put all these perspectives together in our design of the Detox Prism framework, to reiterate how these interfaces reveal failures of trust, and why redesign at each interface entails a mix of incentive-reward systems and moral contracts.

A preview of the rest of the book

The first chapter probes one of the core relationships in organizations: the rapport between management, on the one hand, and labour on the other hand. This is a relationship that is rarely analyzed in all its complexity. Dysfunction (shirking by labour, work stoppage, harassing by management, etc.) at this interface explains a substantial amount of the social waste generated as a result of coordination failures.

The important but unheralded work of Harvey Leibenstein on X-inefficiency and elementary game theory is used to guide our analysis. The equally unheralded work on conventions[22] provides keys to practical ways to address these costly management-labour coordination failures. The experiences of Lincoln Electric and of the Result-Only-Work-Environment (ROWE) concept illustrate how some mixes of incentive reward and moral contract have rebuilt trust and worked well in various instances.

The second chapter deals with the more complex interface between the organization and the network of other partners and suppliers it collaborates with in the generation of its products and services. The complexity of contracting and sub-contracting relations, in a world permeated by outsourcing initiatives, generates opportunity for partners and sub-contractors to shirk. Slack (in the form of poor quality or safety of the product or services used in the different portions of the value-adding production matrix) soon generates distrust for the organization *in toto*. These matters are ascribable to the ever greater complexity of interrelations blurring lines of

---

[22] Bernard Enjolras. 2006. *Conventions et institutions*. Paris: L'Harmattan.

accountability, but also to the increasing pressures on sub-contractors to perform ever more cost-effectively. Trust cannot be rebuilt without a refurbishment of effective accountability and new arrangements for the enforcement of standards across the sector.

The cases of the fatality rate of the workforce upgrading cell-phone towers and of the control of the origin of conflict diamonds are used to illustrate the sort of systemic failings that occur and initiatives that have emerged to deal with the problem. They also illustrate the work done to rebuild trust, and the key role that might have to be played by industry associations.

The third chapter examines the toxic interface between organizations and their socio-physical environment. This is an interface that has attracted much attention from economists, who have looked at ways in which organizations externalize or 'dump' on third-parties many of their costs, and thereby generate significant distortions in the matrix of socio-economic production and consumption decisions. Many subterfuges have been proposed to get specific externalities internalized in *ad hoc* ways without much success, but a *melange* of better pricing of externalities, new conventions and changes in property rights may provide a correction to this family of toxicities and thereby ensure a more responsible performance for the organization.

Environmental externalities (plastic shopping bags, carbon dioxide emissions, etc.) illustrate how such correctives might work: pricing of externalities (even at a symbolic level) acting as a signal and raising consciousness, thereby triggering behaviour modification through all sorts of mechanisms (shame, status, reputation, etc.), by leveraging sensitivities that have been developing in the ethos.

The fourth chapter deals with the complex net of relationships around stewardship *per se*. The stewardship and governance of organizations are inquiring systems as a source of wayfinding and social learning, and a system of guarantees (1) that the different key stakeholders' interests will be taken into account; and, (2) that the long term future of the organization is kept firmly in mind in the navigational decisions. This puts a lot of strain on organizations and stakeholders that might be naturally myopic, blind to diversity, averse to uncertainty, and feel most uncomfortable with having to factor in those dimensions.

To ensure effective collaborative decentred governance in time, the stewardship must recognize both (1) the importance of new scoreboards that will echo the interests of the key stakeholders involved, and succeed in mobilizing their active contribution; and, (2) the centrality of moral contracts making up the burden of office of key stakeholders in the stewardship of organizations. Since one cannot abolish diversity and uncertainty, mechanisms must be put in place to ensure fast social learning and to avoid hijacking by any one stakeholder or one group of stakeholders. Concrete suggestions about finessing corporate governance are used to illustrate how more effective stewardship can be achieved through a complement of redesign fixtures.

The fifth chapter deals with perhaps the most challenging of all interfaces: the relationship between the organization (as part of the social order) and the moral order that underpins the social order. Traditionally, these cultural and moral orders have served as a important source of *garde-fous*: Adam Smith, in *The Theory of Moral Sentiments*, stated that men could be trusted to pursue their own self-interest not only because of the restrictions imposed by law, but also because they were subject to *built-in restraint derived from morals and religion*.

With the weakening of the social virtues in modern socio-economies,[23] this moral vacancy has had some significant crippling effects on the social order, and led to important organizational failures as a result of the imperium of sheer logistics. Such failures have brought back on the scene discourses about the legitimacy of moral references in daily life. Thus we explore the ways in which the notion of multiplex

---

[23] Fred Hirsch. 1976. *Social Limits to Growth.* Cambridge, MA: Harvard University Press.

value adding and the language of integrity may be allowed to impose restraint anew on the social order.[24] The special role of honour codes is mentioned.

The sixth chapter shows how an integrated view of these five interfaces – what we refer to as the Detox Prism – provides an alternative perspective of the meso-organization as a complex adaptive system, hints at a new appreciation of the processes of organizational and institutional evolution, and gauges the promises and limitations of the organizational redesign artillery in mitigating the harms of toxic coordination failures and in ensuring a better stewardship of organizations.

This new perspective is based on a systematic effort to lift the observer with the skyhook of a crane (1) to *broaden* the outlook to take into account not only the narrow focus on individuals but also their circumstances; (2) to *lengthen* the time horizon to take the future into account; and, (3) to *elevate* the perspective point in order to escape from the strictures of the contingent circumstances and to get access to realities beyond the surface of things.

In closing, the chapter suggests a tentative list of issues that should be given priority in the research agenda that would seem to follow naturally from the *problematique* developed in this volume.

The conclusion offers appropriate praise to the unheralded design function and to design thinking in this detoxification work, and speculates most prudently on the contours of the refurbished organization of the 21st century.

Coda

This project could not have been brought to fruition without the support of the Centre on Governance of the University of Ottawa over the past few years.

We are also grateful to clients and partners who have shared their concerns and knowledge with us and have allowed us to make use of their experience to bolster our argumentation. We have been immensely careful not to make

[24] Gilles Paquet, 2011b, chapter 4.

use of sensitive information or of any markers that would have allowed these concerns to be identified, but it should be clear that we would not have been able to develop this book without their generous support.

Finally, we would like to acknowledge the professional help of McEvoy Galbreath and her team at Invenire Books for seeing the manuscript through the publication process with great skill.

Feedback from readers would be appreciated. We can be reached at the following emails: gilles.paquet@uottawa.ca and tragan@cviewstrategies.com.

| X-inefficiencies: the interface of management and labour

The first problematic zone of coordination failure is the interface between management and labour. This interface has changed dramatically over the last century. We are no longer in the 'Taylorian' world where the division of labour into fragments demanded little initiative from relatively unskilled workers, who could be regarded as easily replaceable parts in the production system.

In a more knowledge-based economy, the modern workforce is made up of skilled workers. They are now expected to adapt and adjust to constant restructuring of the production system as a result of technological change. This entails greater capacity to exert judgment and commitment on the part of workers in a world where globalization puts such pressure on production systems across the world that jobs are forced to evolve more rapidly.

Therefore, the relationship between management and labour is no longer shaped by the sole requirement of the procurement of a brute physical labour force where anyone could easily be replaced by another body; instead it is shaped by the need for labour and management to engage in some form of partnership where trust plays a major role, at the very moment when technical change and globalization make any labour arrangement ever more precarious and contingent.

Even though economists have toyed with the notion of a labour market in search of the sort of invisible hand capable of ensuring effective coordination *in toto*, it has been clear for quite some time that the 'labour market' is a fiction and a fantasy. Labour is not a homogeneous commodity, and it is not traded in a single perfectly competitive market. What exists is a *labour process*, composed of a multitude of segmented *labour exchanges*, each with their own rules and internal dynamics.

From time to time, broad sweeping macro-adjustments may unfold – a tsunami across all major segments of the labour process – as the result of an immense gap between supply and demand materializing across the board more or less at the same time. An instance of it has been the recent economic growth spurt in Alberta that has sent forceful signals that important opportunities exist there at all levels, and has triggered massive movements of workers westward.

However, these adjustments should not be presumed to work continually, freely and smoothly in less dramatic circumstances. Multiple limiting rules (about entry, qualifications and the like) apply to the different segments of the labour process, and ensure that a vast majority of citizens are effectively excluded from entering many of these 'internal' market segments where openings are purported to exist.[1]

Some segments of the labour process may have national scope. Indeed, there may be a reasonable presumption that certain skills may be shown to be fairly standardized and transportable across the land. Consequently, the bearers of these skills are quite mobile across the country, and some segments of the labour process might be regarded as truly 'national.' However, it would be unwise to presume that this should be allowed to underpin the fiction of one market. Most segments of the labour process are more likely to be local or technological fragments than is usually presumed.

[1] Peter B. Doeringer and Michael J. Piore. 1971. *Internal Labor Markets and Manpower Analysis*. Lexington, MA: Heath; Michael Reich, David M. Gordon and Richard C. Edwards. 1973. "Dual Labor Markets: A Theory of Labor Market Segmentation," *American Economic Review*, 63(2): 359-365.

This is ascribable to some significant inertia due to family ties, community networks, linguistic barriers, differential local or regional trade and professional standards and accreditation processes, and the like. Consequently, there are severe limitations on broad-brush policies that ignore local circumstances.

The very fact that the labour process is so balkanized leads one automatically to conclude that one might not be able to rely upon market forces and competition to effect the ideal allocation of labour across labour exchanges. Too many rules, exclusions, blockages, etc., exist for the market to be operating at its best. So the case for market failure is quite easy to make. This is equally true within labour exchanges.

In the rest of the chapter, we proceed in four stages. First, we sketch the nature of the pathologies at the management/labour interface. Second, we probe the sources of the coordination failures at this interface. Third, we identify ways in which the coordination failures might be resolved. Fourth, we propose examples of organizations that have tried to cope effectively with this family of challenges: a particular company – Lincoln Electric of Cleveland, Ohio – and organizations that have adopted the strategy of developing 'result-only-work-environments.'

Pathologies

The labour process is more in the nature of a gridlock: it is an *anti-commons-zone* where tragedy strikes not because of open access and the overuse of the resources (as in the case of the traditional commons), but because access is limited by all sorts of rules. The consequence is that the resource remains underused because of the incapacity to break down these barriers, and to make the highest and best use of the existing human resources.[2]

Because so many segments of the labour process are protected from open competition, there exists, within any particular segment, the presumption that a certain *slack* may exist: labour is allowed to exert a level of effort that is sometimes much lower than it might have to be if there were robust

2 Michael Heller. 2008. *The Gridlock Economy*. New York: Basic Books.

competition. The amount of effort effectively put forth by labour depends on an array of motivations (intrinsic motivations, monetary and non-monetary incentive-reward systems, and related rules, conventions, etc.). So actors may provide more or less effort within certain bounds.[3]

This poses two separate problems of coordination failure.

First, the gap between actual and potential effort may be dramatically important because the arrangements in place fail to motivate members effectively. In some studies, the order of magnitude of the potential increase in effort that might be generated by the right mix of incentives and rules has been assessed as reaching up to 40 percent.[4]

Second, there is also the possibility of a failure of coordination that emerges from another source: the lack of trust between management and labour may generate a prisoner's dilemma type problem – both parties being trapped in a situation of interaction where neither party trusts the other and, as a matter of consequence, it appears to be in the best interest of both parties not to cooperate fully and completely.

Because of the low trust level, both parties are led (1) in the case of labour, to exert no additional effort, even when it could easily do so; and (2) in the case of management, to show no interest in providing either market or non-market incentives or soothing arrangements to get the workers to exert more effort, even when it could easily do so. In the worst cases, whatever the first party may do to entice the other to improve the arrangements, the second party would appear to be able to do better by providing less. This is the dynamics of the interaction *per se* in a prisoner's dilemma problem.[5]

---

[3] Harvey Leibenstein. 1987. *Inside the Firm*. Cambridge, MA: Harvard University Press, p. 47.

[4] Harvey Leibenstein. 1976. *Beyond Economic Man*. Cambridge, MA: Harvard University Press, chapter 3.

[5] The prisoner's dilemma, as an original story, refers to a situation where two prisoners have committed a crime jointly. But the police force has no hard proof. Each is urged separately to squeal on the other. If one turns in state evidence against the other, he is promised a light sentence and the other a very harsh sentence. If both squeal, they receive a harsh sentence. If neither

This has been stylized by Harvey Leibenstein as follows: management may offer richer packages (M3>M2>M1), and employees may exert more or less effort (E3>E2>E1) – these levels corresponding to maximum, average and minimal incentives and efforts.[6]

The payoff for each pair of choices is captured by the two numbers in each cell in Table 1 – the number on the left representing the payoff for employees, and the one on the right the payoff for the management. If both parties have no trust in each other and cooperate least, they choose to offer a minimal package of benefits and a minimal effort, and both parties fare poorly at payoffs 3 and 3. If they have great trust, and allow themselves to cooperate fully, they can give their best possible package and supply their best effort, and both parties would do well at payoffs 7 and 7.

TABLE 1: **Payoffs for diverse options
by management and employees**

		Management		
		M3	**M2**	**M1**
	E3	7\7	4\8	1\9
Employees	**E2**	8\4	5\5	2\6
	E1	9\1	6\2	3\3

Note: Each cell contains x\y where x represents the employee payoff and y the management payoff corresponding to a given level of effort E by employees and a level of benefits M provided by management.

squeals, they both go free or get a minimal sentence. A prisoner's dilemma framework involves a mix of trust and self-interest. Each party is faced with choices that may be represented in the most simplified situation as between trusting his partner not to squeal and narrow self-interest (taking advantage of the situation because one cannot trust his partner at all). When there is no trust, each party, acting out of narrow self-interest, takes a decision that leads to clearly the least desirable outcome for both. This is the situation of mutual distrust.

[6] Harvey Leibenstein, 1987, p. 51.

As can be seen from Table 1, no matter how one side behaves to start with (and this is the crucial feature of the situation), when one examines the possibilities open to the other party, it pays the other party to reduce the package or the effort. For instance, if management provides the richest package to start with (M3), employees can improve their situation by doing less and less. Obviously, this situation can only lead to management's reducing its package, and the game would converge toward E1 and M1.

This "unproductiveness trap" generates very high X-inefficiency ascribable to slack, and it has been shown that the X-inefficiency at this interface is often generating much waste (20 to 40 percent of potential output). The outcome reminds one of the sad situation of labour/management relations in the former Soviet Union, where it was often said by labour leaders "they pretend to pay us and we pretend to work."

This shows that the opportunity cost of not exploring ways to improve coordination at this interface is quite high.

Sources of the pathologies: cheating and shirking

What is crucial in such a situation is the amount and quality of directed effort exerted by human capital that can be extracted by management (1) through motivational incentives, and (2) through ensuring that interactions between management and labour are based on a sufficient amount of trust to guarantee that it does not degenerate into complete coordination failure.

The sources of the X-inefficiency may therefore be separated into two parts ascribable to the two sorts of coordination problems mentioned above, and success in jointly resolving these two problems of coordination (motivation and trust) may be gauged by reference to three benchmarks:

- the extent to which the level of effort chosen by employees can be improved by soundly-designed and properly-operated incentive plans (effective packages of wages and working conditions); this would entail finding the way to ensure optimal pressure and optimal rewards generating effort, quality of work, low absenteeism, etc.

that can deliver the highest and best use of employees (part A);

- the extent to which arrangements (conventions or moral contracts, for instance), complementary to the soundly-designed package mentioned in the last paragraph, might generate the level of trust and *affectio societatis*[7] necessary for both parties to indulge in collaborative endeavours, and not to fall into strategic shirking behaviour that would endanger the viability of this collaboration (part B); and,

- the extent to which these two strategies are not only complementary but supportive of each other and self-re-enforcing (part C).

One cannot deal with these problems separately. It should be clear that the simple use of rich incentives to bribe labour into making a greater effort is bound to fail in the absence of a strategy to develop the sort of cultural change that is required for part B to work. Any workable solution will require both parts acting as blades of a pair of scissors to be effective.

Redesign required: incentive rewards and conventions of trust

Resolving the motivation problem will take the form of a configuration of remuneration, fringe benefits, work conditions and the like, and the package will be greatly influenced by the standards in good currency in the corresponding segment of the labour process. The nature of the package depends on the nature of the issues domain, the context and the circumstances.

---

[7] Vincent Cuisinier. 2008. *L'affectio societatis*. Paris: Lexis-Nexis Litec.

Resolving the trust problem (the prisoner's dilemma problem) requires something quite different that could be defined as "conventions" or "moral contracts."[8]

Leibenstein[9] defines the main characteristics of a convention as "mutual perception by all those subject to the convention of (1) the applicable contexts within which the convention can be followed, (2) agreed-upon variations of the applicable contexts, (3) the appropriate behaviour that indicates that the person is following the convention, (4) agreed-upon variations of the convention, and (5) a sufficiently high degree of adherence so that others believe the convention is being followed."

Some of the life work of Elinor Ostrom[10] has shown that in many cases of common-property resources (where individual self-interest may lead to an overexploitation and destruction of a common-property resource), some arrangements have been arrived at to establish conventions (endogenous rules with graduated sanctions and rapid low cost conflict resolution) that have worked well, and have succeeded in ensuring the sustainability of the resource. This may be regarded as demonstrating the possibility of designing such an endogenous arrangement without the need of an external referee.[11] It should be clear, however, that conventions may

---

[8] Philippe Batifoulier (ed.). 2001. *Théorie des conventions.* Paris: Economica; Bernard Enjolras. 2006. *Conventions et institutions.* Paris: L'Harmattan. In the case of the original prisoner's dilemma, the convention that resolved the problem was *omerta* – a way for the mafia to get gang members not to squeal by promising squealers a fate worse than death. This approach (stripped of its odious aspects) is the general avenue that has been suggested by much game theory work: it has focused on the need to develop conventions and moral contracts to nest management-labour relations into a broader context where the incentive not to cooperate would be minimized.

[9] Harvey Leibenstein, 1987, p. 70.

[10] Elinor Ostrom. 1990. *Governing the Commons.* Cambridge, UK: Cambridge University Press.

[11] Trust being engineered through conventions and moral contracts will be a recurrent theme throughout this book. It will be mentioned in the next couple of chapters when renewed trust is required to resolve problems at the interfaces between the organization and its suppliers, between the organization and its socio-physical environment, or between the

not and need not be entirely endogenous: in some cases, some external refereeing or regulatory work, acting as safe-fail mechanisms, may be required.

Effort conventions, quality conventions, etc. (as determined by negotiations) may be suboptimal, but will have to be agreed upon if the dual sources of X-inefficiencies are to be dealt with.

In the case of the labour-management interface, the problem is symmetrically the exact opposite to the one in the case of a common-property resource discussed by Elinor Ostrom: the issue is to ensure better utilisation of a resource that is likely to be underused because of the blockages mentioned above, rather than overused as a result of the unconstrained access to the limited common-property resource. But there is no reason that conventions cannot be hammered out to ensure more efficient and sustainable outcomes in facing the threats of both resource overuse and resource underuse.

A primer on conventions

Given the fact that the reader is probably much less familiar with conventions than with the package of remuneration, working conditions, and the like – but also because the notion of convention is such a crucial component of the way of resolving coordination failures – not only at this interface but also at other interfaces – it appears useful to develop this notion of convention a bit more fully early in the book.[12]

First, a convention is quite a complicated entity. It is an agreed upon regularity of behaviour that is appropriate to certain contexts. The formulation of the convention is often vague, its origin obscure, its texture evolutionary, its character somewhat arbitrary, and the convention is not necessarily subject to legal sanction.

governing of the organization and the stakeholders. Indeed, conventions and moral contracts will also be at the core of the common public culture that is foundational in sociality and ultra-sociality, and underpins the development of honour codes in chapter 5.

[12] In so doing, we are drawing on the two general synthetic versions proposed in the Batifoulier (2001) and Enjolras (2006) books.

The general shape of relevant conventions has been etched in a most skeletal way by Leibenstein, and we referred to it earlier. But there has been an extraordinarily rich literature emerging from France, in particular, where an array of conventions have been discussed, designed and experimented with. Even a sketch of what the literature on conventions has produced over the last few decades would take volumes. Suffice it to say that it has been found useful in the world of exchange of goods, in labour exchanges, in ensuring the quality of the products, etc. [13]

Generally, a convention can be elicited:

- *either* through a set of norms arrived at through history, negotiation or the like to deal *directly* with the coordination problem by modifying behaviour by mutual consent,
- *or* through transforming the representations or inter- pretations of the different actors of what is going on (by lengthening the time horizon, broadening the contextual knowledge, etc.) to obtain a modified interpretation and *indirectly* a modification of behaviour and, consequently, the needed collaboration.

The reason why the second layer (representations and interpretations) is important is that most of the time the rules embodied in conventions are somewhat incomplete because of their very vagueness and, as a result, require a modicum of interpretation. Conventions need to be interpreted, for they underpin coordination and collaboration, justification, differentiation, etc., and consequently cannot be mechanically applied without first being properly "understood in context." In that sense, in most cases, conventions are not like grammar rules that are meant to apply without much reference to context, motivations, or reasons to act in certain ways, etc. They demand some understanding of the context if they are to be applied wisely.

---

[13] François Eymard-Duvernay (ed.). 2006. *L'économie des conventions*. Paris: La Découverte, volumes I and II.

In the case of meso-organizations designed to be platforms for collective action, coordination has a dual nature – "technical" and "relational" – and entails a mixture of conventions. For instance, in a private firm, employees are focused on the work/ wages relation, and the employer on the wage/product relation. And there will be a need to strike some compromise that will meet the expectations of both parties.

These compromises will partly materialize as a wage/ working conditions labour contract, but will also entail some additional conventions about what is expected from each party if productivity and innovation are to ensue – questions about what happens when unemployment is inevitable, for instance, or how to ensure the requisite organizational learning that is necessary if workforce adjustments are to proceed smoothly in a world where the meso-organization operates in a competitive and evolving context in which long term viability depends on a capacity for collective learning and continuous refurbishment.[14]

Depending on the context within which meso-organizations are nested, the dominant factor in shaping the nature of the conventions may be efficiency-effectiveness, egalitarianism, competition, proximity, prestige, etc.[15] Particular broader "dominant" common principles, echoing the common public culture, shape a macro-corporate-culture within which the meso-conventions are nested.

This broader context will also play a determining role in the adjustment of the conventions and the rules. The evolution of conventions will depend on the fact that they are tangled up with the broader social, cultural and moral dimensions of the context. These ideas will be developed further as we tackle the ways in which conventions might be useful to cope with coordination failures at other interfaces.

---

[14] Olivier Favereau. 1999. "Salaire, emploi et économie des conventions," *Cahiers d'économie politique*, (34): 163-194. A very good example of a simple convention that has been most effective is the *Guaranteed Continuous Employment* moral contract between Lincoln Electric and its employees that is described later in this chapter.

[15] Luc Boltanski and Laurent Thévenot. 1991. *De la justification (Les économies de la Grandeur)*. Paris: Gallimard.

Illustrative cases: Lincoln Electric and ROWE

The best way to illustrate how one might be able to define mixes of incentives and conventions or moral contracts to resolve the X-inefficiency problem is to provide a very short summary of two experiments that have demonstrated general success to date – the case of Lincoln Electric, and the ROWE strategy.

The case of Lincoln Electric

The Lincoln Electric Company[16] is the world`s largest manufacturer of electric arc welding machinery and products. It was founded in Cleveland, Ohio in 1895, and now has more than 6,000 employees in 19 countries, a bit more than half of them in the United States.

There are four key elements in the Lincoln Electric's incentive management system: (1) the use of piecework, (2) a merit-based bonus system that has been on average 77 percent of base pay since 1955, and represents over 30 percent of Lincoln Electric profits, (3) the use of an advisory board made up of representatives elected from the different divisions and an open-door policy of management, and (4) a believable promise of guaranteed (30 hours a week minimum) employment.

Without going into great detail, it would appear that it is the complementarity among these four elements that has made the difference, and ensured high productivity, constant profit, and has maintained Lincoln Electric as a world leader for decades.

For instance, despite the odium attached to piecework (limited margin of maneuverability, skimping on quality, strategic slowdown as fear exists of piecework rates being lowered), Lincoln Electric has been able to counter these potential downsides effectively by allowing work to be individually paced, by defective pieces having to be repaired by the responsible worker on his or her own time, and avoiding skimping on quality because the bonus is gauged on the basis

---

[16] Frank Koller. 2010. *Spark – How Old-Fashioned Values Drive a Twenty-First Century Corporation: Lessons from Lincoln Electric's Unique Guaranteed Employment Program.* New York: PublicAffairs.

of quality, and the worker's bonus can be docked by as much as 10 percent, etc.[17]

Guaranteed continuous employment at Lincoln is explained as follows by Koller:[18]

- It is seen as a competitive advantage for the company.
- It provides covered workers with security against layoffs due to lack of work when the company slows down.
- The plan covers permanent employees in Cleveland (95 percent of Lincoln's US workforce) who have completed three years of service.
- Employees are guaranteed at least 30 hours of work per week.
- Employees are required to work overtime whenever scheduled.
- Workers are not guaranteed a particular job or rate of pay.
- Every employee must be willing to accept transfer from one job to another.
- The plan only covers workers who uphold Lincoln Electric's well-defined performance standards.
- Finally, if the company's survival is threatened by conditions beyond its control – from recessions to natural disasters – the guarantee does not hold.

Quite clearly, the success of Lincoln Electric is based on a mix of incentives (piecework and bonus) that ensures a balanced approach – pressure for quantity with reward for quality – in a manner that would appear to work. Most important, however, is the complementary moral contract ensuring both on-going open dialogue and guaranteed employment. Lincoln Electric is not a formulaic recipe, but only an illustration of the possibility of resolving the two problems at the source of coordination failure at the interface of management and labour – motivation and trust.

---

[17] John Roberts. 2004. *The Modern Firm*. Oxford, UK: Oxford University Press, p. 42-43.

[18] Frank Koller, 2010, p. 60.

Result-Only Work Environment (ROWE)

ROWE[19] is a much more revolutionary approach to workplace culture.[20] It entails a "payment for business outcome contract" where employees are generally managed as self-employed contractors who are only faced with stipulated frequency and expectation of business outcomes. This is a strategy adopted by Best Buy with an average 35 percent increase in productivity in departments that have switched to ROWE.[21] This revolutionary focus on results aims at driving productivity, attracting talent, and increasing employee satisfaction. Evaluations performed by a variety of experts show that it works.

The main challenges are the definition of "expectations", and the establishment of effective "communication" about such expectations on an on-going basis. In a number of companies, adequate metrics were found or invented and the results have been celebrated by those operating under those new working conditions. This most ambitious reconfiguration of the workplace has not yet stood the test of time as Lincoln Electric has, but the new regime has seemingly generated a more efficient, productive and loyal workforce.

Whether the lack of concern about *how* the outcomes are achieved could lead to lying, cheating and stealing remains to be seen. Those concerned about ethical dimensions have expressed their unease. But this may not damn the new regime; it would simply call for a broadening of the conventional notions of expected 'result' or 'business outcome' beyond the traditional Taylorian measures in order to encompass some elements of the *how*.

This trend has already begun to emerge in discussions about value-adding. Recent work has emphasized different ways in which the concept of value-adding can be enriched to take into account the ways used to achieve the results. This may be a necessary extension of the notions that have been

---

[19] See the business case for ROWE on www.gorowe.com.

[20] Cali Ressler and Jody Thompson. 2008. *Why Work Sucks and How to Fix it.* New York: Portfolio.

[21] www.businessweek.com/magazine/content/06_50/h4013001.htm.

used in the past, if ROWE is to be as widely accepted as it is hoped.[22] For instance, the Porter-Kramer enriched notion of shared value-adding can easily accommodate taking into account the ways (social, environmental, moral) in which the outcome was achieved.

This would put some constraint on the "O" of ROWE in order to factor in the sort of socially, environmentally and morally acceptable corridor within which those results can be legitimately obtained.

---

[22] Michael E. Porter and Mark R. Kramer. 2011. "Creating Shared Value." *Harvard Business Review*, 89(1-2): 62-77.

| Escaping fault: the opacity of the production network

One of the economic forces most celebrated since the times of Adam Smith and his example of the pin factory has been the power of the division of labour. By allowing each person or group or organization to specialize in what they can do best, it has been argued that the total production and welfare can be increased. This has proved correct in a wide range of contexts. Yet there is a downside to this atomization of the labour process. As the division of labour proceeds further and further, the larger the number of fragments involved in the production process, the larger the number of interfaces to be coordinated, and the higher the risk of failure in the coordination work.

Early in the last century, it was still possible to tackle the coordination problem with the vertical integration of organizations in one location. The Ford River Rouge Complex at Dearborn, Michigan, was constructed between 1917 and 1927, and achieved continuous work flow from iron ore and other raw materials to finished automobiles. This may not have completely eliminated coordination costs, but it most certainly reduced them considerably by having all of the integrated operations at one location.

Any internal coordination issue like safety or quality problems, or inappropriate corner-cutting, Ford was responsible for. If there were downstream supply chain challenges with the final product, Ford was also responsible for them. This is a clear outcome of having all production phases 'in-sourced,' under one direction and accountability.

It is no longer thinkable to have such a vertically integrated organization today: the opportunity costs of integrating fully all the stages of production in one location would be too high in the new modern economies.

The division of labour has been globalized, and globalization has evolved exponentially. This has made the production process significantly more effective. But the technical and relational coordination challenges have become more and more daunting, and the probability of failures within this complex international socio-cultural production network has also grown exponentially. Massive outsourcing has therefore introduced significant challenges when it comes to determining *who* is to be held ultimately responsible for glitches or coordination failures that have detrimental impacts on society.

Concomitant with the fragmentation of the production process worldwide, two other dynamics have transformed the production process in most sectors: (1) the new imperative of organizations having to meet the demands of ever more heterogeneous and diversified populations has meant that all meso-organizations are being pushed to provide more for less, and have had to be ready to generate an ever greater variety of products and services demanded by an ever more plural and pluralist citizenry; and (2) the acceleration of technical change has not only driven the costs of many inputs lower and lower very quickly, but has also led to expectations that constant modifications and improvements of production systems can be expected. For example, in the case of many business supply chains serving consumer industries, it is a general presumption that suppliers should be able to achieve a five percent cost reduction annually as a result of having got further down the learning curve. A portion of this cost-reduction is, of course, expected to be passed on downstream in the supply chain to that supplier's direct customer.

Combined with the opportunity cost of fully integrating vertically and locally, both the variety imperative and the expectation of constant improvement of the production process (resulting in cost reduction) have made the investment in facilities like Ford Rouge River most unlikely these days. In the present context, the best location for such a complex might change as frequently as every five years.[1]

In order to have an agile organization, it is much easier to build on a broader platform of possibilities (competence-wise, price-wise, quality-wise, etc., – worldwide) to enable constant change, rapid response and higher quality. Such massive outsourcing has called for the replacement of central control that cannot easily and speedily react to flaws and faults at different points of more global organizations. This has entailed making fuller use of the possibilities of decentralization, subsidiarity, self-organization and self-optimization. These new governance processes are more likely to generate cost-effective and variety-full products and services in distributed facilities, corresponding to a division of labour ensuring better harmonization among coordination, motivation, performance and innovation.

Such complexity and fragmentation also emerge even within the bounds of a country or industry as a result of the evolution of the property right regimes: "when too many people own pieces of one thing, cooperating breaks down, wealth disappears, and everybody loses."[2] It generates a "tragedy of the anticommons" – a term created by Michael Heller to make visible the underuse of resources, and the waste that ensues when the fragmentation of a socio-cultural production system is plagued by coordination failures due to such balkanization.

Whether the complexity and fragmentation of the socio-technical production process is ascribable to globalization, to property rights regimes, or other forces, coordination has become more difficult, and coordination failures more likely.

[1] Hans-Jürgen Warnecke. 1993. *The Fractal Company – A Revolution in Corporate Culture*. London: Springer-Verlag, p. 25.
[2] Michael Heller. 2008. *The Gridlock Economy*. New York: Basic Books.

The complexity of the interconnections among organizations and sub-organizations has introduced a great amount of opacity in the networks of private, public and social organizations. It has reached such levels in this network of relationships that it has often become impossible to assign responsibilities, and to be sure that repairs are quickly made in the case of failures. So organizations have been unable to assure their partners and end-product users that they are reliable and resilient, and deserve to be trusted.

Pathologies

The number of cases where tragedies struck, and responsibility was denied by all parties involved, are many: the Firestone and Ford tire controversy in 2000, and the British Petroleum platform explosion in the Gulf of Mexico in 2010 are well-known cases in the private sector, but the tainted blood tragedy in the voluntary sector, and the sponsorship scandal at the Canadian federal government level have generated the same sort of puzzlement at the difficulty in unearthing, from the maze of relationships, the culprits who could be held responsible for the disasters. Whatever inquiry was launched did not seem to get to the bottom of things, and left a sense of things being unfinished.[3]

In all these cases (of which the few mentioned above are only a very small sample), complexity and fragmentation have led not only to a failure to ascertain true responsibilities, but also to much deception. Various groups have attempted to shift the blame around; scapegoating has been the response to mob pressure for producing a guilty party; and the growth of a general distrust for complex organizations has led either to their demise, or to their dishonourable discharge from important duties that they had carried out well and honourably for quite a long time (as in the case of the Canadian Red Cross after the tainted blood tragedy).

The toxic impact of these crises on corporate culture and their aftermath in all sectors has been immense. The often misguided search for guilty parties for these mishaps

---

[3] Ruth Hubbard and Gilles Paquet. 2007. *Gomery's Blinders and Canadian Federalism*. Ottawa: University of Ottawa Press.

has led to a consequent surge of distrust within the broader organizations that experienced these local mishaps. These frictions have been such that some observers of the broader scene have suggested that as much as 20 percent of productivity might have been lost as a result.[4] Perhaps even more important is the fact that the external malefit of one organization being exposed as not worthy of trust (and, in extreme cases, being erased from the map, e.g., Arthur Andersen after its role in the Enron debacle) has had an immensely toxic impact on the industry or sector as a whole. Although distrust in the whole of government, as a result of the Canadian sponsorship scandal has not been measured, and the impact of the tainted blood tragedy (and of the reprehensible way in which it was handled by the appointed commission of inquiry, the police and the Solicitor General of Ontario)[5] on the voluntary sector has not been seriously gauged, it has been palpable.

The same holds true every time an organization fails without a credible and well-articulated explanation – whether it is a Chernobyl-type event, a scare in the food-chain, or a snafu in the voluntary sector that no one appears to be able to ascribe to a clear source. The wicked problem of failure in the attribution of responsibility has generated much concern, but more importantly has considerably delayed the needed repairs.

Users and citizens grow disaffected, support declines, distrust grows, cooperation becomes more difficult and the commitment to the organization vanishes, with the result that some observers have surmised on the basis of their studies (without much violent reaction or contradiction) that maybe it has come to the point where only 20 percent of employees use their full potential at work.[6] This has translated into a significant loss of agility and the capacity to transform for

[4] Hans-Jürgen Warnecke, 1993, p. 182.

[5] It is worth remembering that the 'culprits' chosen by the Ontario administration of justice for the events of the early 1980s were totally exonerated by Justice Benotto in the fall of 2007!

[6] Hans-Jürgen Warnecke, 1993, p. 96. This does not entail that the loss ascribable to employees not making use of their full potential is due to supply chain issues. There are various problems of coordination at the different interfaces.

organizations in all sectors, and greater difficulty in meeting the challenges of the turbulent environment in the face of generalized unaccountability and irresponsibility. Trust has disappeared.

Sources of the pathologies: opaqueness and irresponsibility

The basic pressure point in dealing with the socio-technical nebulae of the production process is "supplier relation." While it can be loosely monitored in a very simple production chain, involving only one or two suppliers, it becomes very opaque when the value chain (or more appropriately, the value matrix) has become a complex net of multidimensional arrangements that involves hundreds and often thousands of suppliers or more – worldwide.

In modern business value-adding supply matrices, these numbers of networked suppliers are not at all unusual, as each step in the supply chain develops a sub-network of outsourcing. While a top-tier manufacturer may have a 'preferred supplier program' with only a few dozen or a few hundred suppliers, each of these preferred suppliers may well have several dozen or hundreds of sub-suppliers, and so on. The supply chain matrices can grow very large and complex, very quickly.

In this sort of world, the strength of the socio-technical system is only as great as the strength of its weakest link. And when it is not clear that each partner will live up to his commitments, it means that the likelihood of some sort of failure is high.

In the best of all worlds, each partner in the supply matrix would be fully aware of the expectations of his collaborators and would be committed to meet them. The sort of moral contract in use would be that the partner would live up to the expectations of his collaborators; if not they would be able to explain why there had been a failure, in terms that the collaborators would find acceptable, and provide an alternative solution.

In such a world, transparency would clearly reveal the source of the problem, and graduated sanctions would materialize when failure occurs in order to discourage insouciance, and correction would be exacted when mishaps materialize.

But we are not in this sort of world. Pressure to deliver exists on organizations (private, public or social), and is applied to all the partners involved. Either the partners are fully committed – and have the competencies to meet new evolving challenges by being creative and innovative – or the partners are not fully committed and, in reality, are incapable of coping creatively with new challenges. In the latter case, partners will shirk, evade obligations, and not meet expectations. This in turn will kill trust, and increase the probability of failure of the whole enterprise.

It may be that particular circumstances beyond the control of a partner will prevent him or her from delivering as promised. However, acts of God, tsunamis, impenetrable and chaos-generating complexity, and the like are not the main source of the failure to deliver. Insouciance, shirking and deception are the most general cause of coordination failures. When such actions occur, the maelstrom of supplier relations often leave the whole picture so opaque that it is very difficult to 'prove' that indeed the failure of partner Z to deliver has caused the enterprise to fail, and so all partners generally suffer.

This has led to new religions focusing on transparency and accountability as panaceas. Yet, as Jean Lacouture would suggest, transparency is to truth what nudity is to love – necessary perhaps but not sufficient to ensure effective and responsible coordination.[7] As for accountability, in the worst scenarios, the pursuit of accountability as an absolute has led to inventing guilty parties even when there are none.

In both cases, it has been felt that insouciance, shirking and deception could be eradicated by "external pressure," and that commitment would emerge as a matter of consequence. This is rather naïve. If anything, the use of external pressure often

---

[7] Jean Lacouture and Hughes Le Paige. 2005. *Eloge du secret*. Bruxelles: Labor, p. 9.

erodes intrinsic motivation. So if one is to be concerned about eliminating or attenuating insouciance, shirking and lack of *affectio societatis* by partners, betting on "intrinsic motivation" might be preferable to counting exclusively on extrinsic pressures.

Redesign required: SP(I)N and intrinsic motivations

If both new contextual pressures and a certain insouciance in meeting the expectations defined by the partners' burden of office are responsible for much shirking, the corrective entails a mix of: (1) a modernization of the governing paradigm, (2) a greater appreciation of the power of a moral contract, and (3) a new role for industry associations and kindred meso-institutions in different issue domains.

There is no way that organizations facing these new realities can be effectively governed either by top-down hierarchical bureaucracies or by simple market forces on the assumption that the earth is flat. Neither of these organizational forms would seem to fit the sort of mingled reality of the new socio-technical production system.

What would appear to become a less inadequate picture of the organizational structure in use is the one proposed by Victoria Hine under the inelegant label "segmented polycephalous network" (SPN), which would look like a "badly knotted fishnet with a multitude of nodes and cells of varying sizes, each linked to all others either directly or indirectly" if one insisted on mapping it.[8]

Hine has compared the structure of multinational firms with this form of SP(I)N where the unifying forces that keep the structure from disintegration are horizontal organizational linkages rooted in "ideology." The "ideological glue" lies in the commitment to a very few basic tenets shared by the partners. These basic tenets that hold the organization together are very much in the nature of elements of moral contracts that define

---

[8] Victoria H. Hine. 1977. "The Basic Paradigm of a Future Socio-cultural System," *World Issues* (April-May): 19-22; Paul Laurent, Gilles Paquet and Tim Ragan. 1992. "Strategic Networks as Five-Dimensional Bricolage" in *Proceedings of the IMP 8th Conference – Business Networks in an International Context: Recent Research Development,* R. Salle, R. Spencer and J.P. Valla (eds.). Lyon, France, p. 194-206.

the burden of office of the different partners, in the manner that emerged with the creation of VISA.[9]

The sort of principles or moral contracts around which VISA gathered originally has been summarized in the following way by Dee Hock in describing a protypical "chaordic organization:"[10]

- equitably owned by all participants;
- equitable rights and obligations;
- open to all qualified participants;
- power, function and resources distributed to the maximum degree;
- authority should be equitable and distributive within each governing entity;
- no existing participant should be left in lesser position in any new concept of organization;
- to the maximum degree possible, everything should be voluntary;
- it should induce, not compel, change; and
- it should be extremely malleable yet extremely durable.[11]

In most sectors, when dealing with the challenges facing an issue domain, the only group that might have the capacity to elicit such arrangements, to secure broad support, and to ensure some enforcement, might be industry associations or similar organizations that have a commitment to the resilience and success of the industry or the sector as a whole, and to its long run survival. Indeed, these are the very features of sound corporate governance.

This three-pronged approach (chaordic governance, moral contracts, and meso-connectors capable of the required intermediation) would appear condemned to meet much opposition: the corporate governance paradigm is quite

---

[9] Dee Hock. 1999. *Birth of the Chaordic Age*. San Francisco: Berrett-Koelher Publishers Inc.

[10] It should be clear that this form of chaordic organization and the moral contracts on which it was built are no longer the driving forces behind VISA. In 2008, VISA transformed into a more traditional corporate form via an initial public offering of almost $18 billion.

[11] Dee Hock, 1999, p. 137-139.

difficult to modify because of its legal skeleton; and the notion of moral contract is quite challenging to use in the case of a multidimensional matrix of partners. So it would appear that the most likely tool that might be usefully leveraged is a family of arrangements emerging from the industry or sector itself, if one is to ensure the viability and survival of the sector by inventing ways to build intrinsic motivations and commitments.

The messiness of this nexus of coordination problems at this interface is such that neat and simple solutions have not been fully developed yet. And when they are proposed and set in motion, the exponential growth of the complexity of relationships has often shown them to be no panacea. The best one can expect at this stage is a broad indication of the direction in which the search or inquiring system for effective redesign should proceed.

The commercial airline industry approach to air safety provides some insights into what an adaptive and continually 'learning' industry might look like. The industry started in earnest serving World War I military and logistical concerns, and, in 1918, the US Postal Service won the right from government to provide air mail service. By the 1920s, passenger services were introduced; however, the take-up was very slow, as there was lack of consumer knowledge and important general public misgivings about the level of air safety in the young industry. At industry's urging, the US federal government passed the *Air Commerce Act* in 1926, charging the Secretary of Commerce with developing air commerce through making and enforcing air traffic rules, certifying aircraft, licensing pilots, and various related activities. Companies involved at the time felt that the airplane could never reach its full commercial potential unless the federal government was seen to be aggressive in developing, monitoring and improving overall air safety standards.[12]

Over subsequent decades, the regulatory and operating framework overseeing air safety has evolved into a most sophisticated global governance system. All planes are

---

[12] Source material: http://en.wikipedia.org/wiki/FAA.

required to be outfitted with black boxes which are self-contained, robust data collection units. All problem incidents are investigated by an independent investigation team, and the black boxes are recovered and interrogated for data collected before and during the incident. Based on the results of this investigation, the investigating team can issue both recommendations and required actions, depending on the seriousness of their findings. All airlines operating those affected aircraft are required to put the required fixes (e.g., new training regime, new maintenance procedure, new operating procedure, retrofit of existing planes, etc.) into place within a strict time limit; failure to do so creates risk of loss of the airline's ability to operate in the commercial airspace.

When starting fresh with a new industry offering (commercial air travel as here, or the case of the introduction of the VISA credit card referred to earlier) presented to an unaware or untrusting public, industry participants are generally quick to recognize that some sort of bigger, systemic approach is required to underpin consumer confidence and help condition the public for embracing the new product or service.

However, what happens when, as in the case of supply chain/matrix complexity, the 'industry' is slowly faced with an emerging problem rather than one that is blatantly apparent, is that overall trust is allowed to be eroded, little by little, with each supply chain/matrix failure.

Unfortunately, in many cases – especially when there is a catastrophic breakdown – the trust is broken almost instantly, leaving all members of the supply complex reeling and bickering over who is responsible for what. This, of course, tends to further erode trust levels.

The challenge, then, is to develop an "inquiring system" that evolves towards an emerging solution hand in hand with the emerging problem.

The problems generated by mishaps in the supply matrix have been widely publicized: melamine in the milk supply has affected a large number of children in China; lead paint used extensively in products built in China for export to the United

States has also generated concern; worker suicides at Foxconn – a major Chinese supplier of Apple – have also attracted much attention. Much of it has allowed the impression to develop that this was 'a China problem,' or at least primarily a problem about industrial and worker safety practices in the developing world.

This is not the case. It is a much more pervasive toxicity, and such systemic failures affect whole industries in the developed world.

Illustrative cases: cell phone towers and conflict diamonds

Two specific cases may illustrate first, the toxic breakdown in a very simple supply chain (cell phone tower climbers) and, second, an example of a long-standing industry (diamonds) with a significant emerging problem that participants have difficulty dealing with – a problem that could dramatically set back the entire industry.

Cell phone towers in the United States

While on the surface it appears to be a very simple and somewhat trivial example, the very high death rate associated with installing and commissioning cell phone towers[13] construction and maintenance in the United States illustrates the problem of supplier network toxicity in North America.

Over the past 30 years, cell phone carriers blanketed that country with cell sites to extend service to the most remote areas. There are now more than 280,000 sites nationwide, up from 5,000 in 1990. Many advances in service require switching out antennas and doing other upgrades, which most often involve a trip up the tower by a worker to physically swap out equipment.

The rapid extension of wireless devices and smart phones has led to competitors having to build the most complete networks as fast as possible. The major service providers have done this primarily through subcontracting (with the

---

[13] The source material for this section is www.pbs.org/wgbh/pages/frontline/social-issues/cell-tower-deaths/in-race-for-better-cell-service-men-who-climb-towers-pay-with-their-lives.

sub-contractors themselves getting involved in sub-sub-contracting) to do the dangerous job of building or servicing these towers. Sub-sub-contractors (often three or four steps removed from the cell phone company) hire at the local level often inadequately trained and loosely supervised workers, operating with unsatisfactory equipment, to do this dangerous job. The growth of the cell phone tower business attracted a lot of newcomers, including outfits known within the business as "two guys and a rope."

Cell carriers have good reasons to outsource tower work: building and maintaining towers, though crucial to cell service, is not part of their core business. Contractors have greater expertise and it is more economical to hire workers where and when needed, given the up-and-down volume of work. But handling tower work this way also insulates companies atop the contracting chain from legal and regulatory consequences when there are accidents. This is the case even though some carriers set prices and timetables for tower jobs, and also set and control much of the technical specifications, including such simple things as how to colour code coaxial cables – but their supervisors typically stay off-site and do not manage the jobs directly.

A May 2012 investigation by *ProPublica*[14] and *FRONTLINE*[15] shows that between 2003 and 2011, 50 climbers died working on cell phone towers sites. Yet cell phone carriers' connection to tower-climbing deaths has remained invisible, as they outsource this type of work to subcontractors. The United States Occupational Safety and Health Administration's (OSHA) database on workplace accident investigations does not list a single cell phone tower fatality under any of the major carriers.

However *ProPublica*'s analysis of OSHA records since 2003 showed that tower climbing has had a death rate roughly ten times that of the construction industry in general. One of the reasons why this work is so dangerous is that time pressure often leads tower hands to use a technique called *free-climbing*,

[14] www.propublica.org.
[15] *www.pbs.org/wgbh/pages/*frontline.

in which workers don't connect their safety harnesses to the tower. This allows them to move up, down and around more quickly, but leaves them without fall protection. In more than half of the tower fatalities, workers were free-climbing, even though government safety regulations strictly prohibit it.

For each tower-related fatality since 2003, *ProPublica* and *FRONTLINE* traced the contracting chain, reviewing thousands of pages of government records and interviewing climbers, industry executives and labour experts. They found that in accident after accident, deadly missteps often resulted because climbers were shoddily equipped or received little training before being sent up hundreds of feet. To satisfy demands from carriers or large contractors, tower hands sometimes worked overnight or in dangerous conditions.

Some cell phone companies claim to require their contractors to follow safety regulations, but there is no incentive for them to know too much about what's happening on work sites.

So the question of how much responsibility large firms have in the behaviour, practices, ethics and working conditions of the sub-contractors they hire remains open.

In the cell tower example, a production system failure may result in delay of the project and death of a worker. In sectors like air transportation, failure may entail the death penalty for an organization. In the latter cases, the 'industry' has been led to develop elaborate processes that have coerced individual organizations into responsible self-regulation by imposing industry standards and very stiff penalties for not meeting these standards.

Such approaches have recognized the need to invent a variety of ways to deal with quite a heterogeneous variety of behavioural faults: restoration, deterrence and incapacitation being the gradual progression for punishment in the face of violation of standards.[16]

These industry-wide approaches, while a marked improvement over no industry-wide approach to these issues,

[16] John Braithwaite. 2002. *Restorative Justice and Responsible Regulation*. Oxford, UK: Oxford University Press.

still have much room for improvement. But it is clear that unless the industry chooses, or is coaxed to develop industry standards for the whole of its network activities, very little will be done to ensure that adequate practices will be adopted across the production matrix.

Conflict diamonds

An example of an industry where some industry-wide effort has been made is the diamond industry. [17]

The diamond industry has historically been a highly concentrated industry with a few well-known multinational players, a strong supply management system in place to help ensure the maintenance of high diamond prices, and an active marketing push to continue to develop demand for diamonds. Generally overlooked in this overall system was the source of raw diamonds, as the industry focus was on the cutting and polishing end of the business, where major commercial value was generated.

From the 1960s onwards, diamonds emerged as a major source of funding for dictators and rebel armies alike through various regions of Africa. Diamonds were ideal for the purpose as they were small and valuable, could be smuggled across borders easily, were generally not highly taxed by national governments as they are difficult to trace and police (and so not monitored and regulated aggressively), and little attention was paid in the industry as to the "original source of the diamond."

By definition, conflict diamonds – often referred to as blood diamonds – are diamonds that originate from areas controlled by forces or factions opposed to legitimate and internationally recognized governments, and which are used to fund military action in opposition to those governments, or in contravention of the decisions of the UN Security Council. They are effectively indistinguishable from their more benign counterparts – legitimate diamonds.

By the late 1990s, a few non-governmental organizations (NGOs) were becoming quite effective at generating a sustained

[17] This case is based on Ian Smillie. 2010. *Blood on the Stone: Greed, Corruption and War in the Global Diamond Trade.* London: Anthem Press.

outcry about how blood diamonds were effectively financing various civil wars and the related human atrocities – use of child soldiers, rape, mutilation and other horrors of war.

The diamond industry responded to the media headlines by generating new codes of conduct and best practices; the next few years brought many pronouncements about changes from the industry, but no actual system changes. An NGO report at the time noted: "De Beers is part of the problem. It is no doubt purchasing diamonds from a wide variety of dubious sources, either wittingly or unwittingly. The breadth of its control, however, is also its major strength and is part of the solution to the problem. If De Beers were to take a greater interest in countries like Sierra Leone, and if it were to stop purchasing large amounts of diamonds from such countries, much could be done to end the current high levels of theft and smuggling."[18]

By 2000, the stage for real action was set: the NGOs had found their voice and were driving the conversation about conflict diamonds. The major industry players (notably De Beers) recognized that they needed to take real action if they were to head off a major catastrophe like a consumer boycott. The UN Security Council and the various UN bodies were starting to awaken to the real connection between ongoing brutal civil wars and unrest throughout much of Africa, the costs to the UN of directly attempting to police those civil wars, and the role of conflict diamonds.

On July 19, 2000 the World Diamond Congress adopted at Antwerp a resolution to strengthen the diamond industry's ability to block sales of conflict diamonds, calling for the creation of an international certification system on the export and import of diamonds, legislation in all countries to accept only officially sealed packages of diamonds, for countries to impose criminal charges on anyone trafficking in conflict diamonds, and a ban on any individual found trading in conflict diamonds. In December 2000, the United Nations General Assembly adopted Resolution A/RES/55/56, supporting the creation of an international certification scheme for rough diamonds.

[18] Ian Smillie, 2010, p. 171.

On January 17-18 of 2001, diamond industry figures convened and formed the new organization, the World Diamond Council. This new body set out to draft a new process, whereby all rough diamonds could be certified as coming from a non-conflict source.

A major milestone occurred with an initiative known as the "Kimberley Process" being introduced to stem the flow of conflict diamonds. The Kimberley Process Certification Scheme (KPCS) imposed requirements on participants to certify that shipments of rough diamonds were conflict-free. After two years of negotiation between governments, diamond producers and NGOs, the Kimberley Process Certification Scheme (KPCS) was created.

The Kimberley Process focuses on stemming the flow of conflict diamonds; it has made smuggling conflict diamonds harder for criminals and has brought large volumes of diamonds onto the legal market. An estimated $125 million worth of diamonds were legally exported from Sierra Leone in 2006, compared to almost none at the end of the 1990s.

Like most things developed by a committee of stakeholders with widely varying interests, the Kimberley Process was somewhat of a compromise. The NGOs had to decide whether to support the creation of an organization with limited teeth, or veto it and possibly settle for the creation of nothing at all. In 2001, a petition signed by over 200 NGO organizations stated:

Self-regulation will not work … All countries involved in the production, movement, and processing of rough diamonds must agree to minimum international standards, and these must be open to international scrutiny. Nothing less will suffice if consumers are to have the confidence they need and deserve … , and all governments have to take responsibility in the fight against conflict diamonds.[19]

The Kimberley Process, as finally agreed upon and enacted, was a voluntary code with limited monitoring mechanisms for an effective certification system.

[19] Ibid., p. 185.

By 2009, a view shared by many of the signatories of the Kimberley Process was that it was becoming ineffective. Most of its members went to considerable lengths to comply with its minimum standards, but, as a regulatory system, its policing was inadequate. Effectively, parts of the diamond industry and some governments were demonstrating that common sense, human rights, and the long-term interests of the industry itself could be trumped by narrow, short-term vested interests. To become effective, the Kimberley Process needs to become an effective and sustainable regulatory system. It requires an independent, accountable, arms-length review system; it needs to have a permanent secretariat with a problem-solving focus; and it needs greater transparency.[20]

* * *

Quite clearly the sort of redesign necessary to deal with these pathologies at the production matrix interface has not been a complete success. In both our illustrative cases, the intrinsic motivation of the major players and of the industry associations has failed to generate what would seem to be required.

It would appear that the research priority in the governance community should focus on the development of an apparatus of inquiring systems and mechanisms of responsible regulation applicable to the different issue domains that could be experimented with by a coalition of the willing. The missing link here is the lack of creative and innovative mechanisms for experimentation.

[20] Ibid., p. 202-203.

CHAPTER 3

| Externalities: the organization and its socio-physical environment

Organizations have boundaries and have metabolic relations with their internal and external environment: the internal environment is comprised of many departments and the like within the broader organization, while the external environment is comprised of other organizations and context in the broader milieu.

There usually exists a sufficient net of communication within the organization to force any portion of the organization to take into account its impact on another portion. As a result, within vertically or horizontally integrated firms that are well run, mechanisms usually exist to ensure that segment A neither cannibalizes nor showers unrequited benefits on segment B, that A takes into account the negative or positive impact on other segments of the firm, and that compensation mechanisms are put in place when necessary.

The relationships with the external environment (physical, social, etc.) are much more insouciant. Every day, products (and by-products of production processes) that are toxic in specific ways are generated and dumped into the external environment, without any attention being given to the third parties that are negatively affected by such activity. Indeed, to the extent that it might be done without anyone's being forced to account for any malefic impact, organizations are routinely tempted to externalize all sorts of costs and allow them to be carried by the environment, another party, or society at large.

When a firm or concern dumps industrial residue in existing rivers instead of paying for their decontamination, there is an externalization of the private costs of doing business onto the public at large and onto the environment, thereby giving such a concern a comparative advantage over other concerns (such as direct competitors) that are paying to decontaminate their own effluents. Such possibilities may well encourage the development of patterns of activity that would not thrive if they had to shoulder the full costs of their operations.

This is even more blatantly the case when a firm is not only surreptitiously discarding a toxic effluent, but is deliberately dumping a lethal product that is unloaded onto an unsuspecting public, even though it is well known that this can generate fatal diseases.

Externalities as pathologies or gifts

The problem has to do with third-party effects or externalities[1] generated by economic or social activities. These spill-over effects take many forms: they can be direct or indirect, they may inflict external malefits on the physical or social worlds, and they may be ascribable to a particular concern, or to many concerns, or to the interaction among concerns.

These external effects are not necessarily negative, although the negative externalities have attracted much more attention because of the malefits bestowed onto third parties without compensation. But positive externalities also exist, such as when some activity of a firm bestows benefits on other firms or the neighbourhood. The unwillingness to pay by those benefiting from activities generating positive externalities also creates a distortion, since such benefits that the producer of the activity cannot capture, and cannot invoice to the third-party beneficiary, entails a disincentive to invest in this sort of beneficial activity. This has been debated, particularly, in the case of public goods from which one cannot exclude citizens

---

[1] Francis M. Bator. 1958. "The Anatomy of Market Failure," *The Quarterly Journal of Economics*, 72(3): 351-379.

who refuse to pay, even though they benefit from it. Well known examples are national defence or public health.

The result in the cases of both positive and negative externalities is a gap between the sort of "accounting on which decisions are made" by private concerns (but also at times by public and not-for-profit concerns) and the "more encompassing social accounting," taking into account the full costs and benefits associated with certain activities. Such a gap has an important impact on investment decisions and important consequences for coordination in the economic system, as a result of the mismatch between private and social costs and benefits. Coordination failure at this interface has been the source of much social waste.

In the case of negative externalities, this has allowed certain economic and social activities to be overdeveloped as a result of their capacity to externalize certain costs (pollution), while in the case of positive externalities, it has meant that certain socially-valued activities have been discouraged by the fact that many beneficiaries could not be excluded from sharing the benefits, but could not be easily and readily charged for them, thereby discouraging investment in such activities (public education).

This externalization of costs (pollution, noise, etc.) leads not only to phenomena that would be generally characterized as private enterprise at public expense, but also to decision makers in organizations electing to incorporate, as much as possible, inputs and outputs whose true costs can be externalized, and thereby generating socially undesirable processes of production.

In some areas where the physical environment has been used as a dump for toxic industrial residue, the harm has been immense including deaths, increase in morbidity, etc. In other cases, the cost externalization has had only minor nuisance impact. The same may be said on the external benefits side: in certain cases, the impossibility of excluding those not willing to pay has meant the demise of socially desirable enterprises, while in other cases, it has simply been a source of frustration without great impact.

In the more complex cases where external effects have been generated by interactions among concerns on a broader scale, rather than by simple spill-over from A to B – like the tragedy of the commons (where irresponsible use of a common property resource can lead to its destruction) – the matter takes on a greater importance and may not be resolvable by simple negotiations between neighbours. It might have to be resolved by a modification of interpretations, a reframing of the rules of the game, or by some cultural changes that modify behaviour.

The global impact of such mismatches between private and social accounts is extremely significant because it has led to the thwarted evolution of the socio-economy – translating not only into less productivity increase and innovation, but also into truly flawed economic structures being allowed to survive and to become an immense liability in the development of national economies.

It should be clear that, while private, public and social enterprises are dynamic and powerful organizations responsible for much of the growth in wealth and collective welfare, they all have a propensity to externalize costs. In most cases, the liabilities and risks incurred in so doing rest with the organization and none with the individuals making the ultimate decisions for the organization. So, while one may wish to point to design flaws in scoreboards and accounting systems as problematic, one should not minimize the perverse impact of the 'limited liability' components of the statutes defining organizations (as we shall see in chapter 4), and the ever more opportunistic behaviour of individuals immunized from responsibility in organizations (as we shall see in chapter 5).

Sources of the pathologies: inadequate arrangements

At the source of the pathologies ascribable to externalities more narrowly circumscribed, one may find three major causes: (1) an incomplete or flawed regime of property rights, (2) inadequate scoreboards to gauge the performance of meso-organizations, and (3) the non-existence of adequate pricing of externalities.

These three factors are closely intertwined in a cascade: often, it is because the property rights regime does not recognize a vast array of liabilities, and that organizations can continue to ignore these dimensions in their scoreboards and performance reviews, that they have been able to successfully fight any effort to price the externalities generated.

For the time being, this vacuum has allowed most of the environmental, social and ethical third-party impacts of the operations of meso-organizations to be routinely ignored. It has been easy to do so when these dimensions are not fully recognized in the legal framework that often constitutes the only binding rules acknowledged by organizations.

Except in very special circumstances, when massive external malefits have hurt a large number of people who were able to communicate their plight through the media – major oil spills for instance – not much has been done to compensate the maligned parties and to modify the behaviour of the organizations that have generated such malefits.

There has been no truly credible and widely acceptable evaluation of the waste and inefficiencies generated at the economy-wide level as a result of externalities, and of the extent of the environmental, social and ethical harm generated, but one can only surmise that it is phenomenal.[2]

The complexity of forces at play in generating externalities means that it is unlikely that action can be triggered on all the three fronts at once. Moreover, it is not obvious that waiting until the regime of property rights and the refurbished performance scoreboards are in place to attempt to nudge the system ahead could be effective in the short run. Consequently, what would appear to be called for in the face of such an array of root causes is "efforts to use shortcuts" – interventions that would try to modify behaviour directly by incentive rewards, and by attempting to use them to allow some moral contracts

<hr />

[2] For instance, the 2006 Stern report on the economics of climate change has conjectured that without action, the overall costs of climate change (assumed to be largely ascribable to earthly activities) will be equivalent to losing at least 5 percent of global gross domestic product (GDP) each year forever!

and conventions to kick in, that might have an impact on the mind of citizens.[3]

The complexity of this interface with the external world is akin to the complexity of the interface with the (supply matrix) internal world of the organization that was examined in the last chapter. But the advantage on this second front is that there is less opacity. Malefits are often more easily observable, or at least detectable, from the outside and, therefore, the incapacity to completely escape scrutiny makes the harm less easily concealed.

At least this is the case for the environmental negative externalities. In the case of social or ethical externalities, measurements are often more contestable, the attribution problem more difficult, and the dollar-value compensation for the malefits easier to challenge, so progress on those fronts might be slower.

Another advantage when dealing with external malefits (as opposed to the internal malefits like those associated with supply matrix problems) is that there has been an emerging tradition over the last half century that has legitimized the use of the price system to deal in part with the problem. While there are quibbles about the ways in which such arrangements can be implemented, the principle has by now been accepted as sound. This has already generated a cottage-industry of externalities evaluation, and of invented "shadow prices" to be attached to them.

There is, however, a downside to this advantage. It is that some ideological currents have come to "sacralise" externality pricing as the panacea.

As we have seen in earlier chapters, while monetary or price arrangements play a key role in mechanisms designed to repair organizational dysfunction, it is unwise to presume that they can do the whole job. Operating in a most imperfect and uncertain environment, there is often the need for non-price elements in effective arrangements. We have

---

[3] This would entail making the highest and best use of existing sensitivities developed over time either by catastrophes or by public education.

made the case for the central importance of moral contracts in this context.

So both elements are necessary and complementary in the sort of new organization redesign that is required. For instance, the new environmental sensitivity that has evolved over the last few decades – and that has underpinned the citizens' willingness to get involved in recycling activities, for instance – has been a cultural phenomenon that has often allowed inconsequential price incentives to leverage such sensitivities to produce a significant multiplier effect for price incentives that would have had next to no impact on their own.

Redesign required: prices and sensitivities

Despite the fact that externality pricing is only part of the solution, the first step in any approach that is likely to trigger results would appear to be the pricing of externalities, for when these spill-over effects are priced, they provide a signal. Most organizations (private, public and social) will naturally oppose such pricing, but once they are priced, organizations quickly adjust their scoreboards and, with a lag, the property rights regime becomes *de facto* transformed.

However, in parallel, there must also be work done to nudge the organizations into accepting a better appreciation of the various dimensions of value adding. Indeed, without efforts to recognize the environmental, moral and social burden-of-office of organizations and of their agents (and therefore the liabilities attached to it) *vis-à-vis* society at large,[4] and to develop greater sensitivities to these dimensions in the corporate world, the exercise of externality pricing will often be a contraption that has no more meaning than the pricing of indulgences.

This is where the Schön triad strategy,[5] that technology, structure and theory have to evolve if organizations are to change, becomes enlightening. Even though to change the technology in order to modify the structure on the way to a change in the theory may seem to be the easier road (and

---

[4] Michael E. Porter and Mark R. Kramer. 2011. "The Big Idea: Creating Shared Value," *Harvard Business Review*, 89(1-2): 63-77.

[5] Donald A. Schön. 1971. *Beyond the Stable State*. New York: Norton.

therefore, that it is through a pricing technology that the behaviour and structure of organizations will evolve and that, as a consequence, and with a lag, the law will recognize this new reality and mend its ways, and the theory of what organizations are about will change), it might be wiser at this time to put the cart before the horse.

Encouraging a rethinking of the theory of organizations to make them more responsive to their various contexts might help (together with technology changes) to make some required structural changes more palatable.

This is going to be particularly useful given the fact that some of the technologies (like the primitive nature of the accounting system in use in North America) will be defended forcefully by professional guilds that have been in practice since the 16th century.[6]

An accounting system, that has been allowed to generate a most reductive outlook on the performance of meso-organizations, puts forward annual reports that are at best antiquated, and at worse perverse as guiding documents. But, getting meso-organizations to factor in many more dimensions of 'performance' than the simple rate-of-return on capital invested, will not be easily accepted unless new sensitivities are born and fostered that might help nudge it a bit.

Challenging the accounting profession as antiquarian, and insisting that families of more comprehensive scoreboards exist that could do a better job,[7] might be more effective if citizens' sensitivities to social, environmental and moral dimensions of the operations of meso-organizations were getting more generally accepted. *De facto*, this challenge to the profession about the organizations' burden of office would probably accelerate the process of rejuvenation of the analyses

---

[6] Alfred von Martin. 1944. *Sociology of the Renaissance*. London, UK: Kegan Paul, Trench, Trübner & Co.

[7] Jacques Perrin. 1977. "Comptes de surplus. Pour un nouveau tableau de bord," *Revue française de gestion*, (11): 35-40.

of performance that would be called for by the introduction of pricing technologies.[8]

This is a world in which one may expect the insurance and re-insurance industries to play an important role as harbingers of things to come. Realizing that they may be on the hook for massive insurance claims, as a result of external malefits, they may be expected to increase the costs of their services and to force their clients to start taking into account some of the potential risks that have heretofore been ignored.

Over the last decade, there has been a slow evolution of expectations from meso-organizations about a multiplicity of bottom-lines having to be considered in evaluating the performance of concerns. However, this exercise remains quite capricious, and will continue to be unimportant until externalities are priced **and** the environmental, social and ethical dimensions are seriously taken into account by the general public. Until both elements materialize (prices and sensitivities), there is little hope that a variety of new organizational forms (like flexible-purpose corporations) that better fit the various circumstances of the modern socio-economies, will become truly popular.

These sensitivities are rooted in the common public culture, and the common public culture, in turn, evolves in ways that depend a great deal on the social and the moral order. These forces shape the nature of the moral contracts between the citizenry and families of organizations. In the world of hyper-modernity, two quite different forces pull in different directions. On the one hand, there is a drift toward cultural and moral relativism that fosters a certain cynical philosophy of irresponsibility and anything goes; on the other hand, a loss

---

[8] As we will see in chapter 4, flexible-purpose corporations (with the potential of formally recognizing a variety of purposes for corporations, and therefore the possibility of immensely more comprehensive scoreboards) have become a reality in Governor Jerry Brown's California in the fall of 2011. This new legal structure is bound to put extraordinary pressure on the accounting profession to develop additional metrics to take into account those additional 'purposes' over and beyond the rate of return on financial investment.

of deference *vis-à-vis* institutions has led to organizations being required to account for themselves more broadly and fully. It is in the tension between these forces that the new sensitivities will take shape.[9]

One may expect that while relativism will prevail at the individual level, accountability at the organizational and institutional levels will become much stricter as distrust increases. This means that one might expect that externality pricing (with an impact de-multiplied by new sensitivities) will drive the organizations to amend their governance and their perspectives in the direction of a more comprehensive appreciation system.

Illustrative cases: environmental externalities

One can expect development first on the environmental front because the sensitization of organizations and citizenry to the environmental footprint has been in progress for decades. In that sense, the public mind has been prepared to recognize that particular family of externalities for a long period. For many, it may have been an unduly long period of gestation, and the strength of the commitment may appear feeble, but a sensitivity has grown that has made the impact of the pricing technology promising. On the other fronts (social, ethical), progress is bound to be much slower, although the recent *Occupy* movement may be a harbinger of a new sensitivity emerging on the social front.

On the environmental front, there would appear to be evidence that the citizenry is ripe for externality pricing. This has been demonstrated with the pricing of the plastic shopping bag. More importantly, one would not be surprised if carbon dioxide emissions pricing might prove acceptable and effective in the intermediate run. Parallel progress on the technology and theory fronts in many organizations is already getting experimented with, as we shall see.

---

[9] Gilles Lipovetsky. 2004. *Les temps hypermodernes*. Paris: Grasset.

Plastic bags now and carbon dioxide emissions later

It is important to realize that the small experiment with charging a trivial price for plastic bags has been successful, not only because of the immediate trigger of pricing, but because externality pricing has been underpinned by 20 years of sensitization about the environment. In fact, the overall change in consumer behaviour – based on only a small pricing change and limited public service announcements – has been remarkable, and has been consistent across various jurisdictions and cultures.

Chinese shoppers – the number one consumers of plastic bags in the world – reduced their consumption of plastic bags by half when stores were forced to charge consumers for the bags. In Ireland, studies record a reduction in use of up to 90 percent.

Can this behavioural change argument be extended to businesses?

Charles Duhigg postulates that before anyone can change their behaviour (habits) they must first be conscious of their current behaviour, and then look to change that by first understanding the cue, routine and reward stages of their particular behaviour.[10]

In the case of charging for plastic bags, the explicit question by the grocery clerk ("Do you want plastic bags? They are $0.05 each.") is the formal trigger that forces the consumer to make a conscious decision about what behaviour they want to exhibit. Regardless of the price set for the plastic bags, the consumer's decision-making process is now a conscious act; the actual price charged for the bags is less important than the fact that a price is explicitly featured. The consumer has been made conscious of a pending decision and will now decide the action they will take. And because of the fact that, for the past decades, we have been increasingly conditioned to make "environmentally aware" choices, it now becomes reasonable for the consumer to make a different choice (not using the

---

[10] Charles Duhigg. 2012. *The Power of Habit: Why we do what we do in life and business.* Toronto: Doubleday.

plastic bags) than in the past, as they have been somewhat educated as to the impact of their choice. And as a consumer is routinely put through this conscious decision-making process, it becomes easier and easier for the consumer to form a new habit of carrying their own reusable bags and forgoing the plastic bag experience. Their reward from their new habit is to feel good about the choice they made by being – at least in a small way – more environmentally benign.

There are good reasons to believe that the concept of carbon pricing might not be that difficult to implement in a business setting. But it should be clear that it would be wrong to assume that it is a matter entirely ascribable to non-zero pricing. What the non-zero price did for shoppers was to act as a trigger for consumers to force the next decision (bags or not?) into their conscious decision-making process. In the case of business, the price signal must be significant if it is to make a difference in their own scoreboard – their financial spreadsheets.

Once there is visibility of some significant non-zero price for carbon emissions on their books, the natural and immediate tendency of all profit-seeking businesses will be to seek to understand their exposure and to mitigate their current and future financial risk by seeking to reduce their emissions, and thus reduce their costs. Essentially, the existence of their estimated carbon dioxide externality, shown as a cost input on their financial models, will force the explicit discussion at the management table: is this a big enough risk that we should worry about it? If so, how much should we worry, and what can we do about it in terms of reducing our risk exposure?

Some firms – specifically large emitters – will immediately start to drive changes in their behaviour because, even with only a nominal price now being visible, they will ultimately decide that the risk inherent in the price rising over time will at some point become material to their business. They will immediately begin to explore more aggressively mitigation/ reduction strategies and technologies that they can marshal in their operational efforts to reduce their costs – by reducing their emissions. Indeed, we are seeing some examples of this in the business environment today, although it is very early days still.

Externality pricing plus: PUMA/Interface

A concerted focus on adding externality pricing to companies' financial spreadsheets will, over time, lead those affected companies to redesign their internal scoreboards to now measure, monitor and, ultimately, reduce their costs of doing business as represented by externality pricing.

One may mention, as illustrations, PUMA (a sports apparel and footwear company with $4.5 billion in annual revenues) and InterfaceFLOR (an industrial carpets manufacturer with $1 billion in annual revenues). In both cases, externality pricing has been a major trigger for taking externalities seriously, but it was not without a big push inspired by complementary forces.

In PUMA's case, they have recently (2010) made an explicit link between their business performance and their externalities by creating an environmental profit & loss (P&L) statement. This was accomplished by estimating all environmental externalities from the company and their associated supply chain partners, and developing a basic price estimate for each externality of note. In this respect, they are a good example of the kind of boardroom/executive suite behaviour one may ultimately expect.

The caveat is that this is a fairly new initiative for them, and consequently it has not yet had time to really become a major driver in their day to day business execution.[11]

InterfaceFLOR, on the other hand, has been on their "sustainability journey" for almost 20 years – since the mid-1990s – and have shown remarkable business improvements while, at the same time, dramatically reducing their harmful environmental footprint. They have become far and away the recognized leader in the emerging sustainability field, and they have made a point of making the information they have

[11] http://about.puma.com/puma-completes-first-environmental-profit-and-loss-account-which-values-impacts-at-e-145-million [accessed October 30, 2012].

learned along the way available to the general public in order that other organizations can learn from their pioneering efforts. They provide routine updates and reports on their efforts to date, and their goal of getting to a zero footprint has ultimately led them to a holistic redesign of their overall business, with environmental externality concerns front and centre in their business design goals.

Interestingly, the driver of InterfaceFLOR's journey, from the start, was the gut level belief of their CEO – Ray Anderson – that business as usual was the wrong path to follow. It wasn't driven at the time by an explicit desire for better economic performance, but by the company's desire to follow a less destructive corporate path.

Ray Anderson's consciousness moment came about from reading a key resource book on 'natural capital.' This led to the decision to realign his perspective on how a successful business should truly operate. Once conscious of the attractiveness of a different business behaviour, Anderson set about redirecting the efforts, priorities, scoreboards and metrics of his company.

*   *   *

The experiences with externalities have been at best mixed. While environmental externalities have been consciously discussed, social and ethical externalities remain somewhat underground. And while sensitivities about the environmental footprint have developed, the resistance to efforts to price environmental externalities remains strong and the number of business leaders that have followed Ray Anderson's lead remains relatively small.

Yet progress has been significant on the three fronts (externality pricing, refurbishment of scoreboards and evolution of property rights), and even more so with regard to sensitivities. Environmental concerns have gone much beyond the economic game and have developed into social and ethical concerns. One may reasonably expect that once the hurdle of the very notion of pricing externalities is fully overcome, the impact of these triggers will be astounding – as was the case with plastic bags – for sensitivities have evolved probably more than has been observed.

On the social and ethical fronts, progress has been slower, but it would be unwise to presume that there has been no progress. The new concern about inequality may reveal a new emerging sensitivity that has not yet found its seductive public expression. But it is percolating – seriously fed by the excesses that we will discuss in the next chapter.

CHAPTER 4

| Hijacking: the challenges of stewardship

T he central feature of the enterprise – whether it is operating in the private, public or social sectors – is innovation and social learning: a capacity to be inventive, ever more productive and value-adding in the broadest sense of the term, and to transform creatively in the face of challenges coming from an evolving and surprise-generating environment – not only by modifying its instrumentation, but also its mission and even its very identity in the process.

This sort of collective endeavour requires effective coordination among the various parties called upon to contribute different assets, skills, competences and activities to the enterprise. This cannot be accomplished exclusively by using market forces and bureaucratic fiats. It requires also (as we have seen earlier) moral contracts defining (even if only very loosely) the mutual expectations of the various parties, and some more or less formal arrangements built on them, so as to ensure the requisite motivation, organization and fair sharing of risks and advantages – the burden of office – likely to allow the concern to adapt, improvise and overcome.

Such composite effective coordination not only deals with the organizational game at a given moment in time, but takes place in a world of production that is continually confronted as time goes by, not only with an evolving and surprise-generating environment, but also, as a matter of consequence, with a variety of changing partners, and an ever changing and evolving texture of the interaction order among partners.[1]

Effective coordination does not automatically materialize in such a turbulent context as a matter of necessity, and whatever stewardship materializes may not generate the requisite wayfinding, innovating and social learning as a matter of course. Governance failures are likely in such a turbulent context. Such failures are ascribable to arrangements that do not effectively tap into the information, power and resources distributed in the heads, hands and souls of the stakeholders taking part in the process of collective creation, and that do not take into account their different legitimate claims fairly – usually as a result of the hijacking of the enterprise by one or more of the partners (shareholders, management, unions, permanent staff, technocrats, etc.).

Consequently, unenlightened decisions are made, and the requisite motivations and propensity to collaborate are eroded even more.

Pathologies

The governance failures of meso-organizational enterprises have been revealed through a variety of pathologies:

- first, a long series of collapses of promising concerns that have failed to ensure the capacity to adapt and learn creatively through intelligent stewardship; and
- second, the abysmal productivity and innovation record of so many organizations and enterprises that may not yet have failed as a result of bad performance, but are on the road to damnation for reasons that have more to do with poor coordination than underperformance of any particular factor of production, or to some ethereal ill-defined force. Governance is clearly at fault.

---

[1] Gilles Paquet. 2011a. *Tableau d'avancement II – Essais exploratoires sur la gouvernance d'un certain Canada français*. Ottawa: Invenire, part IV; Nassim Nicholas Taleb. 2007. *The Black Swan*. New York: Random House.

These pathologies are found in all sectors (private, public, and social or civic). This is very often because they insist on maintaining commitment to a particular *modus operandi* or family of mechanisms traditionally associated with their sort of concerns, at a time when the context has changed. In our baroque world, there is now a need for different integrating mechanisms and new hybrid organizational forms made up of elements borrowed from the different traditional sectors.

This new fluid organizational reality may best be stylized as made up of elements drawn from the three generic ensembles of integrating mechanisms – *"quid pro quo* exchange" (market), "coercion" (polity), and "gift or solidarity or reciprocity" (community and society). Kenneth Boulding[2] used a simple triangle as a mapping device – with each of these families of integrating mechanisms in its purest form at one of the apexes, and all the inner territory representing organizations and institutions embodying different mixes of these integrative mechanisms designed to fit the new baroque environment better.

This new baroque socio-economy has triggered the development of an ever larger number of such "mixed" organizations, blending these different mechanisms to some extent (e.g., market-based public regulation, public-private-social partnering, corporate social responsibility considerations, network governance, etc.) in order to provide the necessary coordination arrangements and orientation maps in a new confused and confusing world. This has translated into a much denser filling of the core of the Boulding triangle: mixed organizations and institutions capable of providing the basis for mediation, cooperation and harmonization – different degrees of "institutional and organizational *métissage.*"

The more complex nature of hybrid organizations has entailed, in turn, more complex stewardship, and greater difficulty in meeting the multiple challenges of integrating all

---

[2] Kenneth E. Boulding. 1970. *A Primer on Social Dynamics.* New York: Free Press.

the relevant partners in the governance, social learning and stewardship of these organizations.

The Adapted Boulding Triangle

Exchange

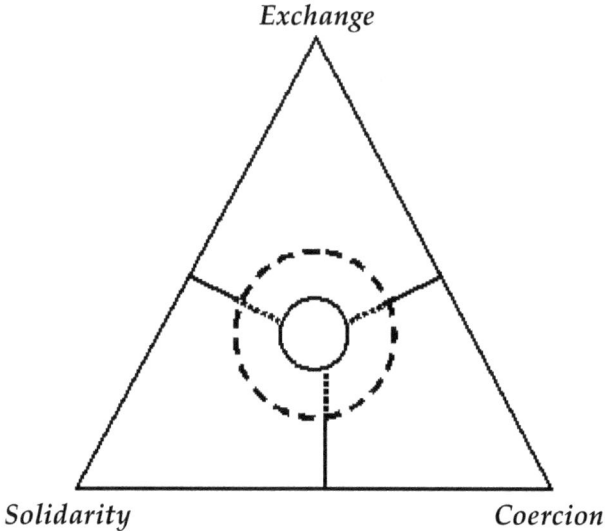

Solidarity   *Coercion*

The central pathologies of governance have emerged from a poor fit between the sort of stewardship necessary in such complex circumstances, and the sort of stewardship in good currency when one or a few partners have hijacked the stewardship process. Such flawed guiding arrangements ensure:

1. neither the effective tapping of the knowledge and information of all those who have a significant part of the resources and power in the organization, or the requisite motivation of those parties so that they can contribute as fully as they can to the objects of the enterprise;

2. nor a determined and forceful focalization on the objects of the enterprise (innovation, social learning, and the resilience of the organization), but rather on the pursuit of a set of narrower objectives to serve exclusively the advantages of those who have hijacked the enterprise.

Skewed stewardship (geared, for instance, to short-term speculative gains by shareholders interested exclusively in share price increases and having no interest in the long-term sustainability of the enterprise) can only translate into governance arrangements being allowed to betray the mission of the enterprise, and to derail its management and strategies in directions that can threaten its survival. Indeed, governance arrangements that permit such abuse of power by one or a few partners are toxic, and when they are engineered or allowed to survive by boards of directors who are complicit in these operations, it may be said that it is the very foundation of our capitalistic system that is undermined.

The perversion of the governance and stewardship of enterprises as a result of its being transmogrified from an engine of collective creation – and a platform of organized collective work – into a simple mechanism to manufacture speculative gains, for instance, is bound to endanger the long term survival of this extraordinary engine of growth.

Sources of the pathologies: hijacking

The core source of pathologies of governance and stewardship in all forms of enterprises is "the hijacking of the process by one partner or the other." In the case of the private sector (on which we focus more particularly for expository purposes), the hijackers might be the financial partners, and the consequent stewarding of the concern being conducted in ways that do not ensure adequate wayfinding, resilience and a fair allocation of risks and advantages among all partners. This derailment may materialize through many governance flaws:

- first, through an "unduly reductive definition of the 'enterprise'" – not as a collaborative inquiring system designed to ensure the capacity to adapt and learn creatively, but as an entity entirely absorbed and represented (according to the gospel of conventional corporate governance, for instance) by legal arrangements clearly unfit for the task at hand because they are entirely geared to the interests of the financial shareholders;[3]

---

[3] Gilles Paquet. 2011b. *Gouvernance – un antimanuel*. Montreal: Liber, part II.

- second, through a consequent "blatant disregard for the contribution of the whole range of partners to the success of the enterprise" in the design of fair and appropriate incentive reward systems likely to ensure their continued creative contribution; this has often entailed a short-term focus on rewarding shareholders and managers (falsely regarded as the sole source of the enterprise success), and a consequent neglect of the long-term investments required in the many other partners, components, segments or compartments of the concern for the enterprise to thrive;[4]
- third, through "a perverse focus of large private enterprises on spending much of their annual proceeds buying back their own shares" to boost the share prices instead of investing in the resilience and creativity of the enterprise; when the fixation on maximizing shareholder values leads to such stratagems, it amounts to stock buybacks as weapons of value destruction;[5]
- fourth, through "a general failure in putting in place meaningful and comprehensive scoreboards" to better gauge the "overall performance" of the concerns when innovation is the crucial challenge, and the requisite motivation and coordination of the different stake-holders are essential for the organization to succeed;[6] and
- fifth, through the "mental prison generated by the 'new' ideology of corporate governance" and the consequent failure to experiment with novel ways of designing organizational forms capable of ensuring the needed stewardship for enterprises in all sectors when they face daunting new challenges.[7]

[4] Blanche Segrestin and Armand Hatchuel. 2012. *Refonder l'entreprise.* Paris: Seuil.

[5] William Lazonick. 2010. *Why Executive Pay Matters to Innovation and Inequality.* Paper presented at the Workshop on Innovation and Inequality, Pisa, Italy (May 15-16).

[6] Mary O'Sullivan. 1998. "The Innovative Enterprise and Corporate Governance." Paper submitted to the European Commission (DG XII) (March).

[7] The idea of the importance of shareholder value is not new, but this has become the overriding and prominent principle that has dwarfed all

These elements amount to a serious indictment of the philosophy of corporate governance currently in good currency.

While the elements above have focused on private sector failures, it is not very different in the public and voluntary sectors: the forms of the blockages are not quite the same, but governance structures and stewardship have been debilitated in parallel ways. For instance, technocrats and "permanent staff" have taken advantage of a certain immunization from competitive forces to steer public and social organizations in ways that served them and their careers much more than the citizens they are purported to serve.[8]

As a result of these governance flaws, two major derailments have materialized: defective scoreboards and flawed frame reconciliation processes.

(a) Defective scoreboards as drivers

The hijacking of the governing process by one or a few partners cannot be easily sustained without a scoreboard that provides legitimacy for this hegemonic team. For instance, the hijacking of limited liability, publicly-traded companies by shareholders has been made possible as a result of the nature of the financial statements that focus quasi-exclusively on returns on capital invested, and do not say much about the many other dimensions of the performance of the enterprise. Reciprocally, the shareholders have been defending this sort of scoreboard as the only meaningful one because it serves them well.

The same holds true in the public or social sectors. The metrics in good currency have been invented by certain stakeholders because they reflect performance as they choose

others over the last few decades. Indeed, it has led, since the mid-1980s, to practices driven by a mindless priority of shareholder value that has been clearly detrimental to the pursuit of the objects of the enterprise (William Lazonick and Mary O'Sullivan. 2000. "Maximizing Shareholder Value: A New Ideology for Corporate Governance," *Economy and Society* 29(1): 13-35).

[8] Ruth Hubbard and Gilles Paquet. 2010. *The Black Hole of Public Administration.* Ottawa: University of Ottawa Press; Gilles Paquet. 2009. *Scheming virtuously – the road to collaborative governance.* Ottawa: Invenire, chapter 4.

to record it. The Management Accountability Framework (MAF) has been invented by bureaucrats to gauge the performance of the federal government apparatus according to standards of efficiency regarded as meaningful by bureaucrats. The same holds for solidarity organizations whose performance is most often gauged by metrics developed by permanent staff and funding agencies to meet their preferred notion of performance.

In general, the metrics in good currency reflect the preferences of the hegemonic partners, and reveal a notion of performance that is in their comfort zone. So when the governance process is hijacked, this will lead to certain scoreboards becoming accredited that may be very poor indicators of the overall performance of the enterprise, but can record the results corresponding to the objectives of the hegemonic partners well.

Modifying the metric is therefore very difficult, because it changes the reference point by which performance is measured, away from a focus on what is of interest to the dominant partner. This entails an interactive dynamic between the dominant partners and the metric: the latter being an important instrument of the former, and providing the basis for legitimacy.

For instance, using the private sector as an illustration, in the case of the limited liability publicly-traded companies, the traditional financial reporting has played a crucial role in legitimizing the primacy of shareholders, and in underpinning the corporate governance gospel in good currency since the 1970s – a new gospel that has sacralised the primacy of shareholders and the CEOs and occluded the other partners in the collective work of the innovative enterprise.

In the 1970s, there was an unseen revolution. Managerialism was challenged, and even blamed, for the decline in productivity, and there was a strong defence proposed for the view that shareholders are principals and that the managers are their agents. This new gospel has become canonical. A variety of reports, commissions and codes have built on this view, and what has ensued is a partitioning of the enterprise as an innovation machine into different components, and a celebration of a segment of the enterprise collective as the only significant and meaningful one.

First, the new gospel reminded the boards of companies that they were accountable to shareholders. Shareholders came to be mainly focused on the value of their shares as the crucial performance indicator. Managers have also been reminded that they were meant to serve the shareholders, and in order to ensure that the managers would comply, many were rewarded for their work by stock options. Consequently they saw their compensation depend more and more on the price of shares on the stock exchange. Indeed, the managers who did not generate such results were merrily dismissed.

Second, the focus on the collective production by the enterprise, and the need to ensure collaboration to foster innovation (a strategy branded "retain earnings and invest"), came to be replaced by a focus on high returns for shareholders. This, in turn, generated a significant distortion of the enterprise project: instead of directing resources to innovation as a matter of priority, a large number of companies have spent as much of their profits to buy back their own shares (to boost their price), as they did on R&D – thereby putting innovation in peril. The whole notion of enterprise has been redefined quite reductively as a "financial investment club" when, in fact, this aspect had traditionally been only a compartment of the work of the enterprise.[9]

These two transformations have led to a significant change in the behaviour of shareholders, who have become mainly preoccupied with speculative gains. As a result, there was an extraordinary increase in the turnover of shareholders – i.e., in the group of persons supposedly choosing the board members to represent them and charged with the wayfinding, resilience and survivability of the enterprise. What was, between the 1940s and the 1970s, "a steady group holding shares" in companies for four to ten years (and therefore interested in guaranteeing their success and viability) has become "a group of nomad investors" holding shares in a company for less than

[9] William Lazonick and Mary O'Sullivan, 2000.

one year, and getting out in order to cash in on short-term speculative gains when share prices increase. This is not only a North American phenomenon but a much broader worldwide phenomenon over the last decade.[10]

This could only lead to the enterprise becoming rudderless.[11] Indeed, it has come to be argued that only the firms with majority shareholders (or a family or restricted groups holding controlling interests, or holding multi-voting shares) could be regarded as having a serious long-term interest in the enterprise *per se*, as opposed to vagrant shareholders being part of the ride for speculative short-term gains only.

The new breed of shareholders (and the governance and stewardship that has come to be elicited by them) has transformed the limited liability, publicly-traded companies into financial machines that have become more and more disconnected from the enterprise that was originally designed to ensure productivity, increase in value-adding, and innovation.

The scoreboards in good currency have been the drivers that led to focusing entirely on rates of return and share prices, paying no attention to metrics taking into account the enterprise's effective coordination and capacity to transform to ensure survivability. Short-run financial objectives came to overshadow completely the long-run objectives of resilience and innovation in the enterprise in a more and more competitive world.

Similar types of chasms emerged in public and social enterprises between the managerial objectives of "efficiency," dictating the behaviour of the technocrats and (more or less directly) their remuneration, and the mission "effectiveness," as defended by elected officials or volunteers intent on tackling social issues of import.

---

[10] Yvan Allaire and Mihaela Firsirotu. 2011. *A Capitalism of Owners*. Montreal: Institute for Governance of Private and Public Organizations, p. 74-75.

[11] Yvan Allaire and Mihaela Firsirotu. 2007. "A qui appartient l'entreprise?" *Forces*, (150), June; see also Yvan Allaire and Mihaela Firsirotu. 2009. *Black Markets and Business Blues*. Montreal: FI Press.

In the case of these public and social enterprises, bureaucratic processes came to impose their discipline and priorities over those purported to provide guidance, and the notion of 'mission' was merrily erased. The hijacking of public and social organizations by bureaucrats and permanent staff was not unlike the hijacking of limited liability, publicly-traded companies by nomad investors and their complicit CEOs.[12]

(b) Flawed frame reconciliation processes

Flawed scoreboards have facilitated this *coup d'état* by nomad shareholders (be they large institutional investors and pension funds) and management entirely mesmerized by the financial dimensions of the enterprise in the private sector (and by bureaucrats and "permanents" in the public and not-for-profit organizations). This has not only left the true enterprise devoid of effective stewardship, but more importantly, in the longer run, the lack of adequate scoreboards has prevented any "effective reconciliation of the different perspectives of the different partners" – a crucial component in effective stewardship.[13]

Partners have different legitimate objectives and wish to have them recognized when the time comes to make decisions about the stewardship of the enterprise. For such a reconciliation of different objectives to be effected, there must be (1) a locus for such definition of trade-offs, and (2) metrics of the broad changes in the performance of the enterprise that would ensue if different decisions were made.

In fact, neither the requisite scoreboard, nor the locus for such discussion to be built on, exists at present. The inadequacy of the scoreboards – and the hyper-focalization of boards of directors on the sole concerns of shareholders – has meant that there can be no real opportunity for the different frames

---

[12] Gilles Paquet. 2010. "Disloyalty," *www.optimumonline.ca*, 40(1): 23-47.

[13] This entails a notion of policy or strategy rationality that goes beyond not only rational choice but even rational politics or negotiation. It entails design rationality and pragmatic resolution of the differences in frames and perspectives *in situ* (Donald A. Schön and Martin Rein. 1994. *Frame Reflection – Toward the Resolution of Intractable Policy Controversies*. New York: Basic Books).

of reference of the diverse partners to be reconciled. Indeed, how could it be ironed out in the absence of any concrete expression of the mission of the enterprise being at the centre of the discussion, and of such discussion being based on a comprehensive picture of the overall multiplex performance of the enterprise.

It is easy to understand why there has been failure to confront this crucial problem in the absence of relevant alternative scoreboards, providing a clear statement of the progress of the enterprise in keeping with its mission, and of a locus where the mission of the enterprise is the object of central attention. Without these basic conditions for useful negotiations, confrontation is pointless, and failure to confront understandable.

What is the point of risking rejection, ridicule, or potential embarrassment, when confrontation in a governance context is tantamount to a "questioning" of many of the parties responsible for or connected with the organizational dysfunction? In the absence of either a philosophy of governance focused on the central mission of the enterprise or refurbished scoreboards that would facilitate discussion by bringing forth the necessary information about performance in the multiplex (social, environmental, ethical, etc,) dimensions of the enterprise, we are, instead, faced with annual reports rationing all information except for the data echoing the rate of return on shareholders' capital and related measures.[14]

---

[14] It may be said that a variety of other information has been added to annual reports over the last while under the guise of the triple bottom line philosophy. However, most often such initiatives have been quite superficial and mainly for public relations purposes. Nothing like what would be required to have a meaningful conversation is made routinely available – something like the sort of *comptes de surplus* in good currency in Europe (Jacques Perrin. 1977. "Comptes de surplus. Pour un nouveau tableau de bord de l'entreprise," *Revue française de gestion*, (11): 35-40) or like what is suggested by the Worldwatch Institute (Allen L. White and Monica Baraldi. 2012. "Reinventing the Corporation" in *Moving Toward Sustainable Prosperity*, The World Watch Institute. London: Island Press, p. 87-103).

* * *

Given these developments, it is hardly surprising that, despite the major challenges, so little has been done to refurbish modern organizations in order to make them depend much more on collaboration and innovation by focusing debates on the surplus generated by the enterprise and available for reinvestment, and how it can best be used to mobilize the creative juices of all the stakeholders. Neither is it surprising that an absence of meaningful efforts to reconcile the different perspectives of stakeholders has led to the demise of many promising enterprises.

The hijacking has taken different forms, and the subterfuges are different in other sectors, but the pattern has been the same: hijacking of stewardship by subgroups, starving of the wayfinding and innovation functions, neglect of any interest in the mission of service (of consumers or citizens), and extraction by the hijackers (shareholders/ managers, bureaucrats or "permanent staff") of significant rewards and rents.

Redesign required: value-adding, scoreboards and corporate forms

In the face of enterprises being stewarded so ineffectively, and of the very erosion of serious concern for the mission, success and survivability of the enterprise in all sectors, three major moves are in order: a new perspective on value-adding, refurbished (even if less precise) scoreboards to better help in stewarding, and new organizational forms.

(a) New perspectives on value-adding

One of the main difficulties inherited from the past in the world of governance is the legacy of management sciences. They have postulated that governance issues pose well-structured problems and have insisted on redefining the "policy sciences" in terms of goals and control. This was immensely reductive. Governance, strategy and policy issues are often by their very nature ill-defined and ill-structured: they must by definition be tackled by "imprecise sciences,"[15] and these issues do not lend themselves to a stylization *ab ovo* in terms of precise targets and goals, and mechanical bow-and-arrow methods to reach them.

Rather, their "ill-definedness" calls for an approach in terms of "inquiring systems" using at best quasi-analytic methods of social learning.[16] A certain degree of imprecision is inevitable, and a reluctance to accept this state of affairs leads one too easily into stylizing the search process into an overly rigid and thereby futile process. The only valid approach is to accept a process based on intelligence and innovation: an inquiring system that feeds a process of social learning. The trade-off here is between more presumed precision in dealing with the caricature of the problem definition, or less precision with a more effective representation of the governance process.[17]

In the case of private sector governance, the guideposts cannot be share prices or rates of return only, but a much more complex ensemble of indicators gauging the result of a combination of "shared value-adding" of the sort explored in a preliminary fashion by Porter and Kramer. In the public sector, the same exploration has generated a line of research about "public value."[18] The same may be approximated for the voluntary sector.

The notion of "public value" (in a most general sense) is collectively built through deliberation, involving elected and appointed government officials and key stakeholders. It leaves somewhat ill-specified the respective role of politicians

---

[15] Abraham A. Moles. 1995. *Les sciences de l'imprécis.* Paris: Editions du Seuil.

[16] Gilles Paquet, 2009, p. 29ff.

[17] Ruth Hubbard, Gilles Paquet and Christopher Wilson. 2012. *Stewardship.* Ottawa: Invenire; Gilles Paquet. 2013. "Gouvernance, science de l'imprécis," *Organisations et territoires* (at press).

[18] Michael E. Porter and Mark R. Kramer. 2011. "Creating Shared Value," *Harvard Business* Review 89(1-2): 62-77; Gerry Stoker. 2006. "Public Value Management – A New Narrative for Networked Governance?" *American Review of Public Administration,* 36(1): 41-57; R.A.W. Rhodes and John Wanna. 2007. "The Limits to Public Value," or "Rescuing Responsible Government from the Platonic Guardians," *The Australian Journal of Public Administration,* 66(4): 406-421.

and bureaucrats (volunteers and "permanent staff"), very much as it leaves unclear *ab ovo* the balance between the various stakeholders in the private sector. This imprecision is however inevitable. Wishing to eliminate it is tantamount to transforming the problem into a simpler and less relevant one.

This multiplex approach recognizes that it is not possible in any sector to aggregate the preferences of all partners in a cardinal way. However, it does not prevent some ordinal and loose ranking of different alternatives. What is important is to focus the attention on some rough guideposts for the social learning process. These guideposts connote once more the notions of moral contract and burden of office: imprecise notions, but notions that are indispensible in defining the roles of each significant partner in the processes of stewardship and governance.

(b) Scoreboards

The sort of general composite guidepost mentioned above cannot be reduced effectively to a simple metric, but it can deploy into an array of indicators that forces the attention onto not one indicator, but a small number of them to be kept somewhat in balance.

This very imprecision entails that no simple maximization of single preference function is possible, but tradeoffs can and must be bargained for, and complementary principles can be brought together in some coherent order.[19]

The *comptes des surplus*[20] is an interesting and more comprehensive way to render an account of the operations of the enterprise in the private sector. It aims at providing a fair picture of the "surplus" (however broadly defined it needs to be) generated by the enterprise, and of the ways in which it has

---

[19] A good example is the dual requirement of fairness (symmetrical) and the importance of the laws of hospitality (asymmetrical) in defining a principled governance approach for immigration policy (Gilles Paquet. 2012. *Moderato cantabile – Toward principled governance for Canada's immigration regime.* Ottawa: Invenire).

[20] Jacques Perrin. 1977 "Comptes de surplus. Pour un nouveau tableau de bord de l'entreprise," *Revue française de gestion,* (11): 35-40; Gilles Paquet. 2008. *Gouvernance : mode d'emploi.* Montreal: Liber.

been used (lower prices, more R&D) in pursuit of the objects of the enterprise – survival, improvement, innovation.

This has the triple merit of:

1. defining the surplus in line with the mandate of the organization (in terms of resilience, innovation and the like, taking into account all the dimensions of performance that are required to ensure the *pérennité* of the enterprise);
2. enabling a conversation about the sharing of this many-faceted surplus, and of the liabilities generated in the production process; and,
3. keeping in mind the "enterprise" (and not only the limited liability, financial-concern component of it) in arriving at decisions about such sharing of the surplus and the risks among all the partners that have contributed to generating the surplus.

It is to be expected that the accountancy profession in the Anglo-Saxon world that has been wedded to the same sort of instrumentation since the Renaissance will resist the pressure to modify the way in which performance is gauged. However, this is bound to be a temporary rearguard action. Already, the more or less informal add-ons to financial statements – under the label of social or environmental bottom lines – have materialized to take into account new dimensions of value adding or destroying. It is only a matter of time before the profession is forced to transform its conceptual framework and instruments. The experience of evolution in Europe, on the occasion of the creation of the European Union and the need to harmonize the status of different organization forms, has provided templates for the new scoreboards.

(c) Transformation of the organizational forms

As for the fuller exploration of all the possible organizational forms for the enterprise, in order to escape the troublesome traps generated by the corporate governance ideology in good currency, (or the parallel surreal fictions in the public and social sectors),[21] it invites experimentation going much beyond the existing legal forms.

This might proceed in two steps.

First: to modernize the existing legal forms by incorporating in the objects of the organization a number of new dimensions of value adding that would appear of necessity to be dimensions of concern; this would formalize what has begun to emerge as issues of interest under the pressure of those who have recognized the creative and innovative kernel of organizations.

This is becoming a reality in California where, in October 2011, Governor Jerry Brown formally ratified the creation of the new "flexible purpose corporation" that could spell out special purposes other than profits as the objects of the corporation. This would help to bring forth a better match between legal status and the more complex reality that has been emerging for quite a while without being granted formal legal nesting.

One can easily see that this greater flexibility might also represent possibilities that can be used by organizations in the public and voluntary sectors.

Second: a more radical proposal might be to reframe the law to accommodate the true nature of the enterprise as a collective creative and innovative concern. This might lead shareholders to voluntarily commit to staying with the organization for a fixed period, labour and other stakeholders making similar types of commitment, and certain arrangements about surplus sharing, à la Lincoln Electric – all this purporting to increase the degree of *affectio societatis*.

Illustrative case: finessing corporate governance

It is difficult in the case of stewardship and governance to find specific concerns that have refurbished their governance so completely that they may be seen to represent an illustration of the way ahead. Some of the alternative forms of governance, like cooperatives, have cured some of the problems but are

[21] Ian Clark and Harry Swain. 2005. "Distinguishing the Real from the Surreal in Management Reform: Suggestions for Beleaguered Administrators in the Government of Canada," *Canadian Public Administration*, 48(4): 453-476.

quite a poor match for most sectors. On the other hand, even new initiatives that appear promising, like the flexible purpose corporation, have not yet had the opportunity to demonstrate their full potential.

Readers interested in both the foundations of collaborative governance in the different sectors and in the various forms of experimentation that have been "wind tunnelled" over the last while can consult usefully the anti-textbook one of us has published on these questions.[22] It examines the ways experimentation has evolved in the private, public, community and municipal sectors, but also at the global level.

But for the purposes at hand, the best way to help the conversation along might be to restrict ourselves to two sketches of action plans that have been proposed recently: the first one is suggesting a significant *bricolage* of corporate governance; the second one is a more ambitious and adventurous plan proposing a true "refoundation" of the enterprise.

Neither plan is likely to be implemented overnight – and the latter may even be regarded as somewhat utopian – but they represent useful stylizations that may inspire much of the conversations likely to fuel the sort of refurbishment that is bound to emerge, in any case, in the next while, given the serious pressures and criticisms that have accumulated about the conventional corporate governance philosophy in good currency.

Allaire-Firsirotu (AF) proposal

This approach takes the form of a list of recommendations to different actors based on substantial analyses and observations by the authors over the years. The succinct list of recommendations presented is not exhaustive, and aims only at conveying a sense of the broad contours of the AF[23] proposed program. Interested readers should refer back to the original pages of their book (168-171) for a complete summary of their recommendations.

---

[22] Gilles Paquet. 2011b.

[23] Yvan Allaire and Mihaela Firsirotu. 2011.

The recommendations we focus on are directed to three families of actors.

1. National governments are urged to:
   - modify corporate law to state unequivocally that the fiduciary duties of the board of directors is to the corporation, not to shareholders, and to permit a different treatment of shareholders on the basis of unequal shareholding periods;
   - support a one-year holding period before a share underpins a right to vote;
   - eliminate favourable tax treatment of stock options, and consider banning them as a means of management compensation;
   - take an active role at the G-20 to impose a tax or fee on speculative transactions; and
   - regulate pension funds to restrict or eliminate their investments in speculative funds.

2. Institutional investors are urged to:
   - restrict the percentage of their assets allocated to speculative investments and refuse to lend the shares of their investment for short-selling purposes.

3. Boards of directors are urged to:
   - make clear that their role is fostering the long-term interests of the corporation;
   - change compensation practices and set a cap on the relationship between compensation of executives and median earnings; and
   - define performance objectives that take into account the more difficult sides of business, as well as the broader social and environmental impacts.

These recommendations (and there are many others) are meant to tame the toxic role of the financial sector; to generate a sharpened sense of responsibility in the different partners in the enterprise; to instill a long-term perspective in its governance; and, to ensure due consideration for the enterprise and all its significant stakeholders.

Segrestin-Hatchuel (SH) approach

This approach puts the emphasis on the need to consider new models of enterprise to get away from the trap into which corporate governance has fallen as a result of the new centrality of "casino capitalism" generated by the reduction of the enterprise to its financial shareholding dimensions, and by the new corporate governance ideology.

Segrestin and Hatchuel[24] examine a variety of alternative models of corporate governance: the cooperative model, the German solution (stakeholders' participation at the level of the plant), and flexible purpose corporations à la California, which are considered, but they also propose a more ambitious model – the so-called "collective-progress enterprise."

The new model is based on four principles:

1. a renewed affirmation of the collective creative mission of the enterprise, and of its central role in generating increasing action and innovation potentialities;

2. a renewed notion of the CEO, empowered to make the highest and best use of the existing potentialities, and to increase these potentialities in the best interests of the enterprise, and not only of the shareholders;

3. the recognition that the different partners are engaged in collective action for the enterprise (some remaining fairly autonomous like suppliers, others being more clearly subordinated to management); and

4. a clear recognition of solidarity in this collective enterprise, with the use of explicit mechanisms that go much further than a simple sharing of profits, but entails a true "mutualization" of risks, and the use of other ways of ensuring that the governing of the enterprise will not allow that decisions permit too uneven a fallout for all partners – including shareholders – including, for instance, the creation of a fund to compensate shareholders for serious drops in share prices.

---

[24] Blanche Segrestin and Armand Hatchuel. 2012. *Refonder l'entreprise.* Paris: Seuil.

The intent is to create new solidarities in collective action inspired from maritime law as it has existed since antiquity and continues to be in good currency: in the case of *avaries communes* – i.e., certain sacrifices suffered in order to save the "enterprise" – all the partners are required to share the burden of the losses in a proportion that is commensurate with what has been saved from perdition through this operation that belongs to them.

* * *

These two scenarios – *bricolage* or "refoundation" – are only proposed as broad ways of exploring the mammoth task of inventing new ways of governing organizations. This is obviously a much more complex task than the ones faced at the first three interfaces. In this latter case, it is not only a matter of "organizational redesign," but one of "institutional redesign": a matter of reshaping the rules to define and change the rules.

| Moral vacancy: the burden/power of sociality and ultra-sociality

M uch of the discussion in the last chapter was built on the recognition that an organization is a nexus of relationships among partners with the purpose of generating shared value-adding through collaboration. It led to identifying problems when the notion of performance was too narrowly defined in terms of the benefits of only a few of the partners, or when the organization came to be hijacked by some partners, and evolved practices that did not reflect the long-term sustainable interests of the enterprise.

Even though the culture and the ethos within which organizations are nested were evoked, these dimensions were only dealt with obliquely. Yet it is clear that the ways in which the governing structures and practices emerge cannot be disconnected from the cultural and moral fabric of the ambient society.

Common public culture (principles, habits, mind-sets, history, lore, etc.) and "sociality" (the capacity to create stable networks) are underpinned by kin selection, reciprocity and norm-conformity (i.e., sympathy, virtue and duty) and lead us to accept certain norms, and to develop a capacity to develop social relations.

"Morality" as "ultra-sociality" connotes taking these pro-social principles and norms beyond the *minimum minimorum*, and applying them in a more thoroughgoing and profound manner. It is the result of our human propensity to norm-conform, and to take into account what is beyond the contingent dimensions of daily life and is anchored in the practice of certain virtues like *prudentia, temperentia, fortitudo, justitia.*[1]

Chapter 4 dealt with the congruence among the views and interests of the various stakeholders in an organization as a means of eliciting a way to appreciate if the rules and principles of stewardship are sustainable, and likely to ensure the resilience of the organization. The present chapter presses further, and raises the question of the "congruence among governance," "culture and morality," that is among:

1. the governance rules;
2. the culture (sociality) or meta-rules – the rules allowing us to change the rules; and,
3. the morality (ultra-sociality) – defining the permissive rules allowing us to change the meta-rules.[2]

Sociality (culture) and ultra-sociality (morality) are not the only factors of import in explaining the evolution of the governance rules. These rules are also modified evolutionarily by logistic, operational, interactional and other forces. However, cultural and moral forces cannot be ignored in defining the corridor of acceptable norms and principles that enables the emergence of satisfactory governance rules.

---

[1] Gilles Paquet. 2011b. *Gouvernance collaborative – un antimanuel.* Montreal: Liber, chapter 4. Charles Taylor. 2007. *A Secular Age.* Cambridge, MA: Harvard University Press has pleaded for the legitimacy of spiritual references and against the devaluation of the spiritual contents of institutions like family and marriage: according to him, they help humans transcend the limits of their particular situation and find a way to anchor their life in a territory beyond the contingent.

[2] These three levels (governance, culture, morality) may be compared to Level I, concern about rules (a law); Level II, concern about meta-rules (the rules to change the rules, i.e., the Constitution); and Level III, concern about the rules to change the meta-rules (in some countries by referendum) (Isabelle Orgogozo and Hervé Sérieyx. 1989. *Changer le changement.* Paris: Seuil). In the present instance, governance rules are the echo effect in part of the culture and morality, and efforts to modify the governance rules cannot ignore the levers offered and the constraints imposed by culture and morality.

Pathologies

The most dramatic source of pathologies at the interface of the organization (making up the whole of the dimensions covered in dealing with the first four interfaces) with the cultural and moral *milieux* is "the growth of cultural and moral relativism" – a sense of anything goes, that these contexts are contingent, and that they should not impinge on the operations of the socio-economy. This comes in sharp contradiction to what was regarded as the necessary contextual norms at the time of Adam Smith. His *Wealth of Nations* could not be read without the parallel teachings of *The Theory of Moral Sentiments* – providing the cultural/moral context that was assumed to prevail if the socio-economy described in *The Wealth of Nations* were to function well.

Modern economics has done much to disconnect the workings of the economy from its cultural and moral surroundings. This disconnectedness has had toxic impacts, for it has allowed some to presume wrongly that the cultural and moral *milieux* have no impact on the workings of economic organizations, and that economic organizations in turn have no impact on the shape of culture and ultra-sociality. Economic historians like Douglass North have shown the importance of this interaction among governance, culture, and belief systems and ultra-sociality.[3]

Vivid examples of the importance of the cultural/moral background on the performance of the socio-economy have been reported by Edward Banfield and Robert Putnam in their studies of modern Italy,[4] and by AnnaLee Saxenian in the United States.[5]

In the first case, it was shown that the northern and southern parts of Italy correspond to very different forms

[3] Douglass C. North. 2005. *Understanding the Process of Economic Change.* Princeton: Princeton University Press.

[4] Edward C. Banfield. 1958. *The Moral Basis of a Backward Society.* New York: The Free Press; Robert D. Putnam et al. 1993. *Making Democracy Work: Civic Traditions in Modern Italy.* Princeton: Princeton University Press.

[5] AnnaLee Saxenian. 1994. *Regional Advantage: Culture and Competition in Silicon Valley and Route 128.* Cambridge, MA: Harvard University Press.

of civic communities, and that their different cultures and moralities tend to explain their governance and their economic and democratic successes and failures. In the second case, the very different culture in California and on the East Coast of the United States are shown to explain how the western group adapted immensely better than the eastern group to major industrial transformations.

In the same manner, the comparison of the performance of organizations and socio-economies equipped with different cultures and moral fibres, or considered as high-trust and low-trust societies or anchored in different ethics, have shown that these features have been important in explaining relative success and failure.[6]

The question is not that a certain culture/morality complex maps necessarily into better performance, but that there are forms of sociality and ultra-sociality that would appear to be more supportive of better performance (however measured), and that mismatches among ultra-sociality (morality), sociality (culture) and governance would appear to be toxic for certain types of organizations. In particular, probing the cultural/ moral fabrics of different national economies (as explored by Hampden-Turner and Trompenaars through a questionnaire to some 15,000 executives) has shown that there may be a certain diversity of mixes that works better than others, and that there is a need for a congruence of some sort among these three dimensions to underpin probabilities of success.

A recent study[7] of some 5,000 managers and executives in the United States that explored the link between the cultural/ moral dimensions of day-to-day behaviour and performance of organizations is enlightening. It discovered that companies fit into three categories: Type I (blind obedience) organizations

---

[6] Charles Hampden-Turner and Alfons Trompenaars. 1993. *The Seven Cultures of Capitalism*. New York: Currency-Doubleday; Francis Fukuyama. 1995. *Trust: the social virtues and the creation of prosperity*. NewYork: Free Press.

[7] Art Kleiner. 2012. "The Thought Leader Interview: Dov Seidman," *Strategy+Business*, (67), www.strategy-business.com/article/12208?gko=5332f [accessed October 23, 2012]. The results of the study have been vindicated in 17 other countries.

relying on top-down command-and control (making up 43 percent of the companies surveyed); Type II (informed acquiescence) organizations that have clear-cut rules and procedures based on rewards and punishments (making up 54 percent of the companies surveyed); and Type III (self-governance) organizations where people at all levels are trusted to act on their own initiative to collaboratively innovate, and common norms and principles guide employee and company behaviour (making up only three percent of the companies surveyed).

It was found that Type III organizations outperformed the others substantially on many fronts:

	Type I	Type II	Type III
Above average			
Financial performance	52%	77%	92%
Reporting of misconduct	26%	62%	94%
Superior			
Rapid adoption of new ideas	18%	67%	94%

The accumulation of oblique evidence of a link between sociality/morality and performance (through a very different shaping of governance) is such that, despite the imprecision and looseness of these relationships, they have come to be regarded as important enough to lead to efforts by organizations to reshape their culture and ethos (even though such actions have proven to take time and to be very difficult) or at least to recognize that the ethos has an impact on performance.[8]

This intermingling of cultural and moral forces has been casually dismissed by those "extreme secularists" (to use Charles Taylor's expression) intent on completely exorcizing any moral dimension from any discussion in social sciences. However, this is an unrealistic attitude. The central forces that shape the burden of office of partners in any organization are

[8] Gabrielle O'Donovan. 2007. *The Corporate Culture Handbook: how to plan, implement, and measure a successful culture change.* Dublin: Liffey Press.

in part inspired by beliefs and morality. Both also contribute to the common public culture, but it is neither easy nor necessary to insist on a neat partitioning of the social and the moral: both matter.

Sources of the pathologies: moral and cultural vacancy

Fred Hirsch[9] was one social scientist who has underlined the crucial importance of sociality and ultra-sociality on economic performance, and the immense cost of the erosion of the cultural and moral underground on which the economic system is built. The same discourse has been heard on the occasion of recent financial snafus, where unbounded greed and outright deception were found to be at the source of many scandals.

The pathologies are rooted in the "unboundedness of the behaviour of individuals and partners" as culture and morals become eroded, with the result that what was accomplished in yesteryear by the practice of the cardinal virtues – *temperentia* (the sense of limits, of not going too far), *justitia* (the sense of what is good), *fortitudo* (a capacity to take into account context and the longer time horizon), and *prudentia* (the sense of pursuing reasonable and practical objectives) – to avoid excesses and maintain a sense of limits, has more or less vanished.

A whole literature has blossomed on the theme of "hyper-modernity." This is the label used to characterize contemporary society – the sort of society that is indifferent to the public good, gives priority to the present over the future, experiences the rise of particularistic and corporatist interests and a loss of the sense of duty and responsibility toward the community. The challenge has to do with the capacity to evolve an ethic of responsibility over irresponsible behaviour in such a context.[10]

This is difficult because hypermodernity has triggered two parallel processes: the growth of individualism, but at the same time the de-sacralization and disaggregation of institutions

---

[9] Fred Hirsch. 1976. *Social Limits to Growth*. Cambridge, MA: Harvard University Press.

[10] Gilles Lipovetsky. 2004. *Les temps hypermodernes*. Paris: Grasset, p. 61ff.

that provided guideposts for the individuals. Such processes do not necessarily generate nihilism, but trust is eroded. It becomes variable, volatile, unstable and fluctuating depending on circumstances.

In such contexts, anomie thrives, and individuals become more fragile and fall prey to a sort of "optional morality" that depends much more on emotions than anything else. It is in this sort of context that an extraordinary relativism opens the way to the most bizarre and unpredictable excesses as a result of the disappearance of any stable meaningful reference points.

This anomie not only relativizes morality, but it also erodes the broad notion of "common public culture" (CPC) that encompasses the whole range of constraints on behaviour, from the simplest acts to the noblest aspirations – some entirely dependent on sociality, but others rooted also in ultra-sociality.

Gary Caldwell has defined the CPC and its constraints at four levels:[11]

1. Manners: etiquette, conventions, and the like
2. The rules of the game: liberties, rights, duties, virtues
3. Fundamental principles
4. Essential beliefs

Together these define a sort of hierarchy of matters on which our *vivre-ensemble* is constructed.

All of them have been eroded somewhat over the last while, thereby dramatically attenuating the capacity to tame our passions by habits and institutions – which are habits *writ large*.[12] This erosion has permeated the whole edifice from the most superficial (though quite revealing) level – etiquette and civility – to the ultimate inspiration of the whole edifice – essential beliefs.

The vacancy left has more or less tended to eliminate inhibitions in the face of any notion of "propriety" and to legitimize a philosophy of "anything goes."

---

[11] Gary Caldwell. 2012. *Canadian Public Culture*. Ste-Edwidge: Fermentation Press.

[12] Joseph Tussman. 1989. *The Burden of Office*. Vancouver: Talonbooks, p. 20.

Cultural and moral relativism are only the deepest elements of this edifice (because they pertain to such fundamentals as personal responsibility and the intrinsic worth of all individuals), but the erosion of this underground has also entailed the erosion of the "overground" – the respect for the rule of law and of basic civility which is the etiquette of democracy.[13]

Indeed, politeness and civility are nothing more than the expression of the first ring in the ladder of virtues.[14] So the four levels cover the whole range from the most elementary virtue at the most concrete level, to the most transcendent, at the spiritual level.

The erosion of this whole edifice of virtues formerly transmitted from one generation to the next by social institutions, and of the whole edifice of the common public culture, has been a phenomenon that has been under way for the last decades – and there is no way in which simple technical adjustments are likely to generate the needed corrective measures.

Redesign required: cultural and moral corridors
Cultural and moral relativisms are the result of some dramatic drifts that have eroded the cultural and moral corridors that were keeping organizations within bounds. But it would be unwise to presume irreversibility too readily, even though these drifts have been forceful for the past 60 years. There is also nothing necessarily unidirectional in the causal chain within this edifice. All those elements are interlinked in complex ways, and cohere, but efforts to bring back a sense of limits at one level may often be triggered by breakthroughs at different levels.

When reflecting on the sort of redesign required for reconstructing a sense of limits and responsibility, one would be wise to start with what would appear to have been the prerequisites for major institutional change in the past.

---

[13] Stephen L. Carter. 1998. *Civility – Manners, Morals and the Etiquette of Democracy*. New York: Basic Books.

[14] André Comte-Sponville. 1995. *Petit traité des grandes vertus*. Paris: Presses Universitaires de France.

On that front, K. Anthony Appiah has proposed an intriguing hypothesis. According to him, many crucially important institutions of the past could evolve only after a revolution had transformed "what is regarded as honourable" in that society. He suggests, for instance, that it was a necessary first step before slavery could be abolished.[15]

Between the moment when an awareness of the negative impact of an arrangement takes hold, and the moment the law or the formal underpinning of this arrangement can be changed, there has to be "a moral and cultural revolution" redefining what is honourable and not. This can come forth in a variety of ways and as a result of the most unforeseen circumstances. But most importantly, it can also come about through a variety of emotional channels: something may come to be regarded as dishonourable as a result of shame, of pride, of reputational capital, and the like, and therefore as the result of a variety of situations.

In the case of business enterprises, sensitivities may be such that there is already much new thinking that drifts in this direction. It is now regarded as inappropriate by many groups to act in ways that are environmentally, socially and ethically irresponsible, and already new legal forms have emerged as a result of this new code of honour.[16] So, to the extent that something as ethereal as the code of honour might be an important game changer, reframing the debates around a new code of honour may represent a promising gambit.

Changing the notion of what is honourable is neither easy nor formulaic. And it need not be based on directly modifying an essential belief on the road to transforming reprehensible behaviour. It need not be a revolution in the mind triggered by deep theory, either, but simply an emotional reaction to some specific feature of the present situation that would transform perceptions or interpretations.

---

[15] K. Anthony Appiah. 2010. *The Honor Code – How Moral Revolutions Happen.* New York: Norton.

[16] Gilles Paquet, 2011b; Blanche Segrestin and Armand Harchuel. 2012. *Refonder l'entreprise.* Paris: Seuil.

Existing regimes have also proved vulnerable to the most innocuous changes. For example, in a francophone high school in Quebec where schoolyard bullying and violence was problematic, some professors suggested that imposing the use of *vous* instead of *tu* in all interpersonal exchanges on the whole territory of the school ground might help. It worked marvelously, even though no one could really explain fully what made it work. Reintroducing a sense of civility in this most perfunctory way tempered violence dramatically.

The challenge, therefore, is imagining ways to reintroduce a sense of responsibility and a sense of limits, and nudging back behaviour within cultural and moral corridors by way of redefining what is the honourable thing to do.

The strategy likely to be most effective would appear to be based on two well-established and empirically-tested propositions.

First, there is the well-known Kohlbergian theory that suggests seven stages of moral development, defining stages of moral progress[17] and decisions being made on the basis of:

0. impulsive amorality;
1. punishment avoidance;
2. calculated self-interest;
3. so others will see you as a good person;
4. to abide by law and authority;
5. to abide by moral contracts; and
6. to abide by the principles of justice, fairness and universal rights.

Second, there are the empirical results showing that studies of executives of private, public and social organizations show them to be located around levels 3 or 4.[18]

On this basis, one might conjecture that through intervening to modify perceptions and representations in the interaction order – and modifying the sense of honour – one might expect

[17] Lawrence Kohlberg. 1981. *The Philosophy of Mortal Development: Moral Stages and the Idea of Justice.* San Francisco: Harper & Row.
[18] David J. Fritzsche. 2005. *Business Ethics: A Global and Managerial Perspective.* Boston: McGraw-Hill/Irwin.

to be able to modify the behaviour of executives in such a way as to bring it to level 5.

Illustrative case: a new sense of honour as lever

The best way to help the conversation along is to explore how one might combat cultural and moral relativism by toying with honour codes, since this would appear to be something that could prove to be a tipping point.

Although much could be done through incentive reward systems and moral contracts at some interfaces, in the case of this fifth interface, the blockages are at the beliefs and principles level – and therefore the currency is quite different. It is unlikely that partners or participants "from the outside" could be "bribed" into abandoning essential beliefs (so closely bound to identity) and submitting to new ones. The trigger is more likely to work through "internal motivations" that challenge essential beliefs, and the behaviours they underpin, by making them suspect, embarrassing and borderline dishonourable.

This has been the strategy of the environmentalists who have, over the last few decades, made it reprehensible socially and morally to ignore the third-party effects of certain behaviours. It is not the 5 cents charged for shopping plastic bags that can explain the extraordinary decline in the number of such bags used: rather, it is the fact that such behaviour has come to be made to look irresponsible, and therefore disreputable, dishonourable.

Changing the sense of honour may not be easy, but it is not as intractable as is assumed. It is a matter that will have to be dealt with primarily at the level of "serious play" with moral contracts and reputation – and with the help of experimentation and prototypes – to counter the flawed beliefs and relativism in good currency.

As we have mentioned earlier in a note, prototyping would appear to be the main activity underpinning serious play:

- identifying some top requirements as quickly as possible;
- putting in place a quick-and-dirty provisional medium of co-development;

- allowing as many interested parties as possible to get involved as partners in improving the arrangement;
- encouraging iterative prototyping; and,
- thereby, encouraging all, through playing with prototypes, to get a better understanding of the problems, of their priorities, and of themselves.[19]

The purpose of the exercise is to create a dialogue (creative interaction) between people and prototypes. This may be even more important than creating a dialogue among people alone. It is predicated on a culture of active participation that would need to be nurtured. Such a multi-logue between people and prototypes allows assumptions that one is not aware one is making to become explicit, and discussions about potential corrective contraptions and mechanisms to be carried out less painfully than what would be the case in interpersonal confrontations.

An experiment of the sort was the study conducted by the Bouchard-Taylor Commission in Quebec on the nature of reasonable accommodation between newcomers and the base population. It is not so much the report that was produced as the outcome of the work of this commission that was of import – the ill-inspired report was shelved – but the conversation triggered by the commission has transformed the public discourse. It is now permissible (most of the time) to have a serious discussion about immigration and diversity and the moral contracts to be negotiated with newcomers (e.g., about things that are not negotiable for newcomers who wish to come to live in Quebec) without being tarred as nativist or fascist – a situation that contrasts greatly with what prevails in English Canada. It has come about through a change in what is perceived as honourable in such discussions in Quebec.[20]

---

[19] Michael Schrage. 2000. *Serious Play*. Cambridge, MA: Harvard Business School Press.

[20] Gilles Paquet. 2008. *Deep Cultural Diversity*. Ottawa: University of Ottawa Press. Changing the mindset of Canadians on these issues by informing them and generating the 'unlearning' required about the disinformation and propaganda inflicted on the population over the last few decades will require such a multi-logue, and a slow and careful approach, for the beliefs in good currency are deeply rooted and any attack on them anathema. For a discussion of the necessary strategy to transform these perceptions and beliefs, see Gilles Paquet. 2012. *Moderato cantabile – Toward principled governance for Canada's immigration regime*. Ottawa: Invenire Press.

To the extent that some reasonable view is seen as defendable in conversations about contentious or wicked problems, it soon becomes a view that others feel they might have to accept in order to retain their reputation of being of sound mind. This oblique way of addressing beliefs may not lead to a dramatic alteration of essential beliefs overnight but, as in the examples examined by Appiah with dueling and slavery (that did not disappear overnight), the reframing that ensues is very much as the result of some modification in the sense of honour, broadly defined.

For our purposes, three on-going strategies might identify loci of such mind-changing import: one in the small, another in the large, and a third one through the use of *catastrophisme éclairé*.

Broadening the notion of value adding

There has been much discussion about the notion of value adding, and it has led to a broadening of perspectives and a better capacity to appreciate meaningful cultural and moral constraints that were camouflaged in the conventional notion. A more comprehensive view of value adding and value sharing is emerging.[21]

An inquiring system has been launched around this question, and one can expect that some refurbished notion of value adding will transform the evolving nexus of relationships among partners and contributors, bringing forth a new view of the organization as a locus of co-learning that the relationships engender, and redefining the corridor of what is acceptable – to ensure its outcomes are both desirable and viable.

This cumulative process of learning and "unlearning" is bound to lead to system modification, development and redefinition over time as more appropriate cultural and moral corridors for the behaviour of publicly traded companies, for instance, will be defined. It will take time but, as noted in the last chapter, there are already signs that the refurbished notion of value adding has led to the creation of new organizational forms.

[21] Micheal E. Porter and Mark R. Kramer. 2011. "The Big Idea: Creating Shared Value," *Harvard Business Review*, 89(1-2): 62-77.

The very concept of value adding has already permeated the public and not-for-profit sectors, and it has generated platforms where new corridors are being negotiated.[22]

From an age of entitlements to an age of responsibility
Some essential beliefs are broadly shared in the community, and even more deeply rooted in the ethos as a result of decades of programming. They are likely to be more difficult to unlearn.

For instance, over the last 50 years, being on welfare has come to be regarded quite differently – it has gone from being considered as somewhat shameful and dishonourable to being regarded as a right. Beneficiaries who lived in shame are now willing to fight for what they now regard as their entitlement, even when claiming entitlements reveals much irresponsibility and self-indulgence. This has accompanied the drift toward hyper-modernity in Canada, and especially in Quebec, where a new ideology (under the label of the Quiet Revolution) has shaped the mindset of citizens and underpinned *une culture de bénéficiaires*. A no-fault all-entitlement society has ensued.

Reversing this process and re-instilling a sense of responsibility will be a Herculean task. It will mean, for instance, making abuse of the social welfare system as a source of dishonour. In a more general way, it would mean changing the way in which citizens perceive their burden of office, and force them to relearn that rights are granted as a way to ensure that citizens are able to fulfill their duties.

Such massive transformations of the moral and cultural basis of a society have been experienced in the past when it has been faced with the challenges of war or defeat. What has to be engineered is the moral equivalent of a war or the sociological

---

[22] In the case of the public sector, see Gerry Stoker. 2006. "Public Value Management – A New Narrative for Networked Governance?" *American Review of Public Administration* 36(1): 41-57; in the case of the third sector, see Caroline Andrew, Ruth Hubbard and Gilles Paquet (eds.). 2012. *Gouvernance communautaire : innovations dans le Canada français hors Québec.* Ottawa: Invenire.

equivalent of a defeat, by way of discussions that will modify perceptions, interpretations, expectations and behaviour.[23] This will entail harnessing not only the force of reason, but also the power of emotions, pride and reputation, and a relearning of the burden of office by the citizenry.[24]

Catastrophisme éclairé

In such difficult tasks, there may be a need to use shortcuts. One of them is intervening to make the worst-scenarios less likely by forcing the attention of partners and stakeholders on the inescapability of disasters and catastrophes. This approach is designed to counter our capacity for denial, and to force agents to take the matter seriously.[25] Too often, potential calamities are readily dismissed and discounted on the ground that either it will not materialize, or technological change will deal with it. By brandishing the worst-case scenario à la Cassandra, as the inescapable destiny, citizens are forced to pay attention and governments are forced to deal with the issue.

This sort of strategic intervention at the level of representation may sound manipulative, but in a world where the attention of citizens and governments is so difficult to capture, it may be a necessary tool of last resort to awaken a population that has developed an immense capacity for cognitive dissonance. Indeed, it might best be regarded as a call to arms when there is a likelihood of disaster. However, one should not feel re-assured that such a device of last resort will necessarily bring forth salvation: Cassandra was always right, but nobody ever listened to her forebodings.

---

[23] Charles P. Kindleberger. 1978. *The Aging Economy*. Kiel: Institut für Weltwirschaft.

[24] Joseph Tussman. 1989. *The Burden of Office*. Vancouver: Talonbooks.

[25] Jean-Pierre Dupuy. 2002. *Pour un catastrophisme éclairé*. Paris: Seuil.

CHAPTER 6

| Putting it all together: constructing a Detox Prism

This book has proposed a somewhat different approach to the challenges created by organizational failures requiring design responses. We have identified five particular interfaces (within the organization, and between the organization and its external environment most broadly defined) where pathologies may be readily detected. We have then probed each of these interfaces in order to uncover some of the important sources of these pathologies, and looked into the sort of redesign action or the sort of levers that might help to make these interfaces dramatically less toxic.

To achieve a certain degree of generality in our inquiry, we have attempted to stylize somewhat the nature of these pathologies, and to hint at broad redesign strategies – and even at inquiring systems – likely to lead to effective interventions, rather than always focusing on specific recipes to deal with very particular difficulties. But we have also presented a few particular cases where specific families of design remedies would appear to be successful, and indicated certain directions for repair work which would appear to be warranted. This was meant to underline that our general argument can be of practical use.

What has been missed in this balkanized approach to the different interfaces is the fact that the pathologies detected at these particular loci do not exist in complete isolation one from the other. Problems at interface A may have an impact on interface B – as when externalities make the production matrix even more scrambled. Moreover, some dysfunction at interface E may be much more toxic than other dysfunctions at other interfaces because of its asymmetric impacts on the whole system – as might be the case for moral relativism. While it was useful for analytical purposes to deal with each interface separately, their interaction is crucial at a time when the necessary redesign is explored.

In this chapter, it may not be possible to unscramble as completely as we would like the structure and functioning of the "generic syndrome" that might explain most of these different pathologies. This will require further work in our ongoing research program on collaborative decentred metagovernance. But we provide a provisional sketch of this syndrome, of the character of the dynamics that underpin it and tend to produce harms in so many directions, and of the general philosophy that has led to the array of redesign strategies that we have proposed in the earlier chapters.

There are four stages in this process.

First, we remind the reader of the crippling epistemologies in good currency in the social sciences, and make the case for a more open-ended and prudent approach in terms of inquiring systems. Second, we synthesize the main features of our approach along these lines to gain a fuller appreciation of the centrality of the common public culture and virtue in the sort of reconfiguration necessary to attenuate harms. Third, we suggest that this approach has allowed us to change the landscape somewhat, and to suggest a consolidated diamond perspective on this cluster of issues – what we refer to as the Detox Prism and provide as a rough-and-ready diagnostic tool. Fourth, we hint at the outline of the integrated perspective that ensues, and at the research agenda that it suggests.

Crippling epistemologies

Failures of governance are most often the direct result of crippling epistemologies.[1] The reductive perspectives generated by these crippling approaches are mental prisons that prevent one from gaining fuller and richer appreciation of the complex realities. As a result, representations of complex realities from these reductionist belvederes are often chromos from which most of the essential dimensions of socio-economic realities in time and space have been excised. For simplification purposes, the models in good currency routinely factor out time, memory and history, but also context and a myriad of dimensions that disciplinary gospels declare extraneous – either because of ideological blinders or because they cannot be measured precisely. On the basis of such cartoons, and an unwarranted amount of arrogance about what may legitimately be inferred from them, disciplinarians propound their infallible edicts. This is often akin to sorcery.[2]

In fact, inquiry in social sciences has to be much more modest, be satisfied to build on the design of inquiring systems that make a minimal number of assumptions, and accept as few non-negotiable axioms as possible. Such inquiries build on social probing, exploring and learning, and focus on anomalies discovered along the way that draw attention to untoward matters likely to reveal tensions, and calling for corrective action.

Unfortunately, the hyper-stylization of traditional analyses has led to much blindness to anomalies, and to slower social learning. As a result, critical thinking has been weakened, dominating ideas have not been challenged, views in good currency have been immunized from scrutiny, and promising new avenues remain unexplored.

[1] Gilles Paquet. 2009. *Crippling Epistemologies and Governance Failures – A Plea for Experimentalism*. Ottawa: University of Ottawa Press.
[2] S. Andreski. 1974. *Social Sciences as Sorcery*. Harmondsworth: Penguin.

Our focus on inquiring systems, on process, and on design[3] – with its insistence on the process of experimentation and prototyping with both new means and new objectives along the way, and on the great probability of failures – invites observers to approach issues differently.

Our approach in this volume is experimentation with inquiring systems, focusing on organizational failures and key sources of dysfunction, and on redesign work that might attenuate the malefits ascribable to these failures and dysfunctions.

The need for a crane

This need for novel and more open perspectives has acted as a forceful motivation to develop "cranes" (to use the language of Richard Normann)[4] which send down a hook to lift the observer into a position where new realms are visible that could not be imagined from aground, allowing a broader and richer perspective.

Our cranes are neither universal cranes, nor the only cranes imaginable, but they have:

1. "broadened" our perspective to take into account inter-actions (social domain), mind frames (cognitive domain), ecological and power interfaces;
2. "lengthened" our time horizon to take into account a more extended future and the possibility of learning our way out of predicaments; and,
3. "elevated" our perspective point to take into account the common public culture within which meso-organizations are nested, and even what is beyond the contingent aspects of the lives of partners in organizations – the transcendent.

There is no standard blueprint for crane construction, but some principles have been proposed by Normann to meet the challenge of designing useful cranes. The crane must be capable of:

---

[3] Ruth Hubbard, Gilles Paquet and Christopher Wilson. 2012. *Stewardship*. Ottawa: Invenire.

[4] Richard Normann. 2001. *Reframing Business*. Chichester: Wiley, part V.

- taking stock of the context and of the mega-community;
- upframing – that is, redefining the out-boundaries of the system one is in;
- moving boldly into future scenarios;
- aiding in wind-tunneling any prototypes that may emerge; and
- signaling the sort of improved competences, collaboration and organization design improvements required.

Our cranes have thrown light on five zones of tension (X-inefficiencies at the management-labour interface, escaping fault at the value-adding matrix interface, externalities at the socio-physical environment interface, hijacking at the governance interface, and moral relativism at the interface of the organization and its social and moral contexts) – zones in which much dysfunction was shown to depend on lack of trust.

Pathologies were shown to be potentially corrected in part by modifications to certain necessary incentive reward systems. But even though such modifications may be necessary, they never seemed to be sufficient: fundamentally, much was shown to depend as well on developing conventions of trust and other moral contracts.

The view from these cranes has revealed that the problem of moral vacancy, at the interface between the organization on the one hand, and the common public culture and the moral fabric of the broad context on the other, plays a crucial role in the emergence (or not) of conventions as a way to resolve the basic problem of trust at all the other interfaces as well. This has made the fifth interface a very special one.

The Detox Prism: a diamond perspective

We may refer to the general perspective from the sky-hook as a "diamond perspective": all five dimensions being of concern, but the fifth one playing a linchpin role in the whole *problematique*.

The diamond approach suggests that much of the redesign work in the first four interfaces depends on what is possible and feasible at the fifth interface – the cultural-moral interface. Unless there is a way to counter the important cultural and moral relativism that has permeated the ethos over the last 50 years, simple plumbing or mechanical contraptions will never succeed in fully establishing a surrogate basis for the sort of trust on which conventions and moral contracts of all the other four fronts depend.

This draws attention to the linkage between the "individualistic" coordination based on agents' individual incentives (in markets, obligational networks or hierarchies) and the "collective" forms of collaboration, based on appeals to solidaristic principles and collective goods[5] (monitoring networks, coalitions, associations of all sorts) more or less firmly anchored in institutional arrangements.

One cannot expect individualistic coordination to emerge in the same form when the collective context is a rich or impoverished institutional arrangement, or if the society's common public culture imposes rich or impoverished normative constraints.

This perspective is synthesized in Figure 2.

This means that repair work cannot be concentrated exclusively on local circumstances and contraptions, but an eye must be kept on the broader circumstances to determine what can and cannot be put in place with any possibility of success – given the cultural and normative texture of the milieu. A great variety of sensitivities and enabling resources are at play in Alberta and in Quebec, very much as they are in France and the United Kingdom, and in California and Texas. They constrain the range of conventions and moral contracts that can be viable in support of adequate incentive reward systems at each interface in these different locations, but they also underpin and leverage a range of such moral contracts.

This is bad news for the compulsive socio-economic operatives who fail to recognize the fundamental importance of the cultural-moral dimension, for their imaginative incentive reward work may be futile and even counter-productive, without the moral contract component of the repairs. But it

[5] Rogers Hollingworth. 1993. "Variation among nations in the logic of manufacturing sectors and international competitiveness" in *Technology and the Wealth of Nations*, D. Foray & C. Freeman (eds.). London: Pinter, p. 301-321.

is good news for those who count on such cultural-moral dimensions to construct design responses to the challenges we have noted.

FIGURE 2: Visualizing The Detox Prism

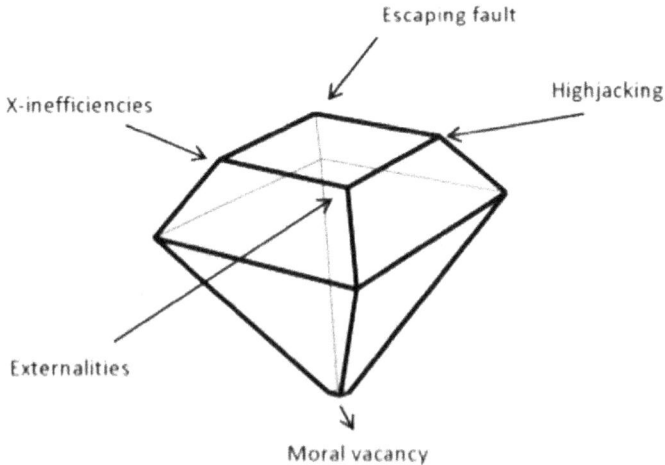

This is, finally, quite a challenge for a group that had hoped that it might be sufficient to rebuild foundational trust in the organization through an accumulation of limited conventions in the other four corners to resolve the overall moral relativism problem. We may be in a situation where nothing but bootstrapping will do.

Those interested in bootstrapping have gained much inspiration from the recent work of Samuel Bowles and Herbert Gintis on the origin of cooperation in the human race.[6] Their work argues that the human species has experienced a co-evolution of its culture and genetics that has developed its capacities to allow the emergence of pro-social norms of behaviour, to institute them in more or less formal arrangements, to internalize such norms, and to form groups contributing to the facilitation of cooperation.

[6] Samuel Bowles and Herbert Gintis. 2003. "The Origins of Human Cooperation" in *Genetic and Cultural Evolution of Cooperation*, Peter Hammerstein (ed.). Cambridge, MA: MIT Press, p. 429-443.

For them, there is a "basic capital of solidarity in humanity" that can be counted on. When one adds to this basic capability the capacities depending on the development of a "common public culture" and related virtues, it leads to the conclusion that there may be a more promising building ground for trust, solidarity and cooperation than has been usually presumed.

This new cosmology developed by Bowles, Gintis et al.[7] builds not only on the gene-culture co-evolution, but goes beyond the contingent by exploring how social emotions (and the internalization of norms built on them) are underpinning moral cognition and the transmission of moral pro-social values.

Such human emotions as shame, guilt, pride, empathy, reverence, integrity, or a sense of honour cease to be delegated to an ethereal out-there sphere of the "moral" inspired by god-like forces, and become arguments of the preference function that the individual develops at the interface between the cultural and the moral.

In contrast to the conventional approaches in social sciences that have often led to reductive views about the landscape, and to futile attempts at carpentering mechanical contraptions that have proven useless or toxic, this new cosmology opens new vistas.

The map changes the landscape

This line (used as the sub-title of the book by Richard Normann) reminds us of both the trappings of our current system of beliefs and norms, and also of the power of transformed cosmologies. Changing the map changes the landscape. This is why cosmology is better than plumbing as a starting point. This is most certainly the view from our cranes.

The focus on pathologies at certain interfaces has revealed the centrality of distrust at the core of all these pathologies, and

---

[7] Herbert Gintis et al. 2005. *Moral Sentiments and Material Interests*. Cambridge, MA: The MIT Press; Hebert Gintis. 2009. *The Bounds of Reason – Game Theory and the Unification of Behavioral Sciences*. Princeton: Princeton University Press; Herbert Gintis. 2011. *A Cooperative Species – Human Reciprocity and its Evolution*. Princeton: Princeton University Press.

has led us to seek repairs both at the level of incentive reward systems and at the level of building trust and moral contracts – trust being the foundation or the dynamic precondition for sustained relations and coordinated communities.

At each of the interfaces, the temptation to rely on ruses, subterfuges and manipulative devices to detox the relationships has quickly faced major limitations. Such devices work only if the pre-condition of trust either exists, or is being built by a cultivation of commitment making and keeping, of reciprocal dynamic relationships developing into *affectio societatis* – not as a means to an end, the medium through which something else can be obtained, but truly as an attitude and a virtue.[8]

The traditional cosmology based on the ultimate dominance of self-interest denounces talk of trust as unrealistic, patronizing and sentimental, and cynically regards trust and commitment as at best a weakness to be exploited in a manipulative way.

In this world, the detoxification of the different interfaces can only come through the design of clever or deceptive incentive reward systems that will guide "rational fools" in desirable directions. Such devices have rarely proved sufficient to detox the interface. In most of the cases, what is required, in addition to certain incentive reward schemes, is the development of trust as pre-condition for sustainable actions to ensure that reciprocal relationships will endure as a meaningful wayfinding in an increasingly complex world.[9]

Recognizing that human beings have a broader rationality than simple means-ends instrumentality, and that they have a capacity for empathy and commitment, opens the door to new levers for change, to the possibility of a detour through the cultural and moral realm to improve the situation at the different interfaces.

---

[8] Robert C. Solomon and Fernando Flores. 2001. *Building trust in business, politics, relationships, and life.* New York: Oxford University Press.

[9] Niklas Luhman. 1980. *Trust and Power.* New York: Wiley; Amartya Sen. 1977. "Rational Fools: A Critique of the Behavioral Foundations of Economic Theory," *Philosophy and Public Affairs,* 6(4): 317-344.

Some may regard this refusal of cynicism and selfishness as a naïve conception of life, but the various cases examined above have shown that a blend of incentive reward and conventions (or inquiring systems designed to elicit conventions) has usually succeeded where Skinnerian incentive machines have failed.

Even more important, perhaps, is the possibility of making use of social emotions and the practice of virtues to refurbish the common public culture and the moral basis of society, in order to repair some of the pathologies at the different interfaces.

Anthony Appiah has shown that many revolutionary changes in the social organization (like the abolition of slavery, or the end of dueling) could only be initiated successfully after a modification in the code of honour – a transformation in the notion of what is honourable behaviour and what is not.[10] It is only after the code of honour has been modified that beliefs, norms and institutions could be transformed.

It may well be that only when we agree to deal directly with the growing cultural and moral relativism, the erosion of the common public culture, and the dismissive and scornful attitude toward the cardinal virtues (or even toward minor virtues like civility), will it be possible to develop the sort of conventions required at the different interfaces examined earlier in this book, for example, on the foundations of some renewed sense of what is honourable in our modern world.

For the time being, the *laissez aller* in all sorts of dimensions, the cynicism that meets all forms of virtues, and the short-term hedonism that is the North Star in our society of entitlements would not appear to have the carrying capacity to generate the conventions required to ensure the needed coordination and collaboration. This entitlement mentality – what makes "a nation of takers" as Nicholas Eberstadt would put it – may indeed be said to be in the process of wasting away "national

---

[10] Anthony K. Appiah. 2010. *The Honor Code – How Moral Revolutions Happen*. New York: Norton.

character."[11] This would appear to put on its head the myth that entitlements are the making of the civic compact. From being considered an asset in the welfare state era, entitlements would have become a liability. Without a renewed notion of burden of office (which is the obverse of entitlements) as a correlate to a new code of honour, it is difficult to imagine that a new landscape will emerge.

A research agenda

Some might say that such a project aimed at detoxifying organizations (at least as we have defined it) is overly ambitious. Many will argue forcefully for nothing as encompassing: for them, *bricolage* should suffice. Our sense is that *bricolage* cannot suffice in such matters, and that that sort of insouciance in the face of the erosion of the cultural and moral infrastructure might be characterized as an "unsettling or rash lack of concern" – the definition of criminal negligence in the Canadian Criminal Code.

Detoxification requires more than superficial sanitization: it calls for confronting the erosion of the ethos so that any repair to the body of governance will be accompanied by a refurbishment of the soul – a replenishment of virtues[12] – in order for the sort of conventions required to be generated in keeping with the spirit likely to ensure their sustainability.

Social sciences, under the shackle of positivism, have systematically strayed from such concerns over the last century. This explains the paucity of the analyses of each of the five interfaces we have explored.

Many recent analyses of the blow-up of the global economy in 2008 have been forced to recognize that the meltdown was the end result of numerous toxic conditions at all the interfaces:

---

[11] Nicholas Eberstadt. 2012. "Are Entitlements Corrupting Us? Yes, American Character Is at Stake," *The Wall Street Journal*, August 31, http://online.wsj.com/article/SB10000872396390444914904577619671931313542.html [accessed October 23, 2012].

[12] Stan van Hooft. 2006. *Virtue Ethics*. Chesham: Acumen.

- faulty compensation schemes;
- atomization of mortgage debt as illustration of supply chain toxicity;
- external malefits inflicted on people and government by a banking sector immunized from constraints because it was regarded as too big to fail;
- governance regime hijacked by nomad investors entirely unconcerned with the long-term interest of the enterprise; and
- moral relativism allowing collaboration to disappear, even though it is an essential ingredient of our socio-economy.

So it is well understood that these interfaces are closely interconnected and that their dysfunctions have generated the meltdown.[13]

However, what has been missed is:

1. the failure to understand the extraordinary limitations of the research done on each of these interfaces with respect to the perverse incentive reward systems and the missing moral contracts; and
2. the failure to understand that the repairs to the dysfunctions at the different interfaces depend on trust, and that the failure of trust depends on vacancies in the cultural and moral realm.

These two blind spots have led too many observers to search for mechanical devices and to indulge in *bricolage* in the way crew members are proverbially said to have been re-arranging the deck chairs on the Titanic when the ship was going down.

At a time when social sciences are at long last rescued from the naivety of some utopian social physics, à la Auguste Comte, what is required is a research program that refurbishes our knowledge base on the five fronts we have explored, and on the new dynamics that makes them so closely intertwined in the explanation of disasters.

---

[13] Gilles Paquet and Tim Ragan. 2012. "The crisis of 2008 through The Detox Prism," www.optimumonline.ca, 42(4), at press.

A provisional list of the sort of research required to both provoke and to kick start the needed conversation on these issues might begin as follows:

A. First, there is a need to introduce much more sophistication in the analyses and discussions of the labour process, and to rescue them from the strictures imposed by the stylized gospels of human resources management and industrial relations; much of the mess in this area is ascribable to the antiquarian frames of reference in good currency that prevent experimentation and effective design thinking.

B. Second, there is a need to free the research on value chains and matrices from the strictures of technology and logistics, when in fact both problems and their resolution depend much more on the "relational dimensions" and on the highest and best use of "communities of practice" and other forms of associations capable of inventing ways to mutualize many of the activities in the value adding matrices.

C. Third, much work is required on the serious pricing of externalities, and on the design of moral contracts; in both cases, there has been much fluffiness in the discussions surrounding these problems, and very little accomplished in providing instrumentation that would be regarded as legitimate by all parties, and sufficiently flexible to match the array of baroque situations one is faced with in our complex world.

D. Fourth, much work must also to be done to explore the avenues opened by the creation of a "flexible purpose corporation" in California; this sort of governance architecture construction site has created the possibility of designing a variety of hybrid organizational forms matching the variety of baroque environments and missions we are confronted with. Moreover, it might be time to flesh out the burden of office of the newly minted CEO intent on serving the purposes of the enterprise *in toto* rather than simply the shareholders.

E. Fifth, there should be efforts to make possible experimentation on a broader scale to deal with broad malaises crippling modern complex societies; up to now these experimentations have been much too restricted to deal with overly specific issues – like the conversations about reasonable accommodation in Quebec. Little imagination has been marshaled to tackle problems crippling the whole of a society, as in the case of the world of entitlements we live in. These experimentations were called for already some 40 years ago.[14]

F. Sixth, much more attention should be directed to the construction of cranes and to the rules that might improve the construction of cranes.

These avenues are not meant to be a comprehensive or exhaustive list of projects likely to be generating important results for the ongoing research and experimenting with the detoxification of our institutions and societies; they are only select broad avenues or platforms calling for further exploration.

Readers are invited to add to this program – in its broad form and in the details.

---

[14] Michel Crozier. 1970. *La société bloquée*. Paris: Seuil.

CONCLUSION

| # In praise of design thinking

The new mindset generated from our crane is built on three important assumptions: the primacy of process, the centrality of design, and the fact that reflexivity and learning loops are consubstantial with any effective stewardship.

These three assumptions of the new mindset are ways to respond to three weaknesses of the old mindset, plagued by (1) its assumptions about a mechanical object-world; (2) its view of decision making and problem solving as occurring within a maze-like world where the problem is purported to be already set; and, (3) a neglect of human intentionality and belief systems in governance processes.

The process approach does not deny that things or objects exist, but it suggests that material bodies and stable structures are rooted in the processes that have generated them, and best understood through an analysis of these processes that remains unfinished and open-ended. It emphasizes a dynamic open-ended approach[1] and builds on reflexivity.

Reflexivity is defined by Bob Jessop as:

... the ability and commitment to uncover and make explicit to oneself the nature of one's intentions, projects and actions and their conditions of possibility; and, in this context, to

---

[1] Donald A. Schön. 1990. "The Design Process" in *Varieties of Thinking*, V.A. Howard (ed.). New York: Routledge, p. 110-141.

learn about them, critique them, and act upon any lessons that have been learnt.[2] Reflexivity means that knowledge acquired gets integrated during the inquiry, and unfolds in order to modify the outcome. This entails a process of inquiry with a built-in on-going critical ability to think about the implications of particular choices, and an on-going capacity to modify means and ends as learning evolves. It means learning how to learn reflexively.

Design thinking

Such exploration leads to learning by doing, and "involves inquiry into systems that do not yet exist."[3] This in turn requires a new way of thinking: "design thinking."[4]

This is a way of thinking that escapes groupthink and convergent thinking, which are designed to "make choices", and favors divergent thinking, designed to "create choices."

The focus of the inquiry shifts from the "exploitation" of existing knowledge to "exploration" for new knowledge: a shift from routine management to the continuous reinvention of the organization, from a refining of arrangements in place to exploration based as much on intuition as analysis, and a shift from short term and low risk to long term and high risk undertakings.[5]

This new way of thinking builds on experimentation, prototyping and serious play, and makes the highest and best use of grappling, grasping, discerning and sense-making as part of reflective generative learning. It bypasses the simple use of focus groups and surveys as rearview mirrors into the future, because, as Tim Brown reminds us, Henry Ford used to

---

[2] Bob Jessop. 2003. *Governance and Metagovernance: On Reflexivity, Requisite Variety, and Requisite Irony.* Lancaster, UK: Lancaster University, Department of Sociology, www.lancs.ac.uk/fass/sociology/papers/jessop-governance-and-metagovernance.pdf, p. 7, [accessed October 23, 2012].

[3] A George L. Romme. 2003. "Making a Difference: Organization as Design," *Organization Science*, 14(5): 558.

[4] Tim Brown. 2009. *Change by Design.* New York: Harper Business.

[5] James G. March. 1991. "Exploration and Exploitation in Organizational Learning," *Organization Science*, (2): 71-87; Roger Martin. 2009. *The Design of Business.* Cambridge, MA: Harvard Business Press, p. 29.

say "if I'd asked my customers what they wanted, they'd have said 'a faster horse'."[6]

Design thinking is a systematic approach to innovation: not being satisfied with managing existing offerings and adapting to new users, but creating new offerings for new users.[7]

This approach is, for the time being, far from being in good currency. In fact, it remains fairly marginal – very much like the Type III organizations mentioned in chapter 5. Most organizations are trapped in mental prisons that prevent them from accepting the open-endedness of the notions of strategies and policies as "inquiring systems." They choose to presumptuously pretend to have all the information, power and resources – and therefore the expertise – to guide their organizations in optimal ways *ab ovo*. Consequently, as experts, they cannot learn, since if they did, it would reveal that they were not experts in the first place.

This is the mental prison from which one has to escape.

There has been in the recent past a flurry of books on organizational design that have brought forth a new sensitivity to the power of organizational architecture.[8] But there is quite a gap between "organizational design" and "design thinking": the former rarely avoids the trap of formulaic recipes, better suited to the construction of ferry-boats that will be used to navigate between the shores of a relatively eventless river, while the latter insists on constructing an inquiring system fit for exploring the high seas, beyond the bounds of the known.

Currently, much time is spent constructing ferry-boats, but there is not much interest in designing ships for high seas exploration, even though the crucial challenges facing governance (if our argument all through this book is accepted) desperately call for design thinking of the latter variety.

[6] Tim Brown, 2009, p. 40.

[7] Ibid., p. 261.

[8] David A. Nadler and Michael L. Tushman. 1997. *Competing by Design*. New York: Oxford University Press; Robert Simons. 2005. *Levers of Organization Design*. Boston: Harvard Business School Press; Richard M. Burton, Gerardine DeSanctis and Berge Obel. 2007. *Organizational Design: A Step-by-Step Approach*. Cambridge, UK: Cambridge University Press.

This brings us back to a difficulty evoked in one of the epigraphs of this book, about the difficulty of waking up someone who is only pretending to sleep.

The challenge is to get observers of organizations (private, public and social) to stop deliberately ignoring the predicaments the old mindset has inflicted on them. This cannot endure, since there is already much grumbling as a result of the failures of the old cosmology in generating useful responses to the present dismal state of affairs. So some awakening will come, followed by a moment of anger.

As Kurt Vonnegut reminds us: "Beware of the man who works hard to learn something, learns it, and finds himself no wiser than before." Bokonon tells us, "He is full of murderous resentment of people who are ignorant without having come by their ignorance the hard way."[9]

So it is only once awakened from this pretended sleep, and rid of a resentment they have until now concealed, that the sleepwalkers will tackle the task of developing ways to construct useful inquiring systems with the help of design thinking.

Quo vadis

What will be the outcome of this design thinking?

It would be presumptuous to pretend that we know what design will characterize the emerging organizations of the 21st century.

We might venture to agree with the modest general propositions that the MIT Initiative on *Inventing the Organizations of the 21st Century Project* has come up with after a decade of serious work.[10] It suggests: that they will be shaped to be environmentally, socially and personally sustainable, that they will be built around different public measures of social value adding and form segmented polycephalous networks, à *la* Hine, integrated by some guiding sets of beliefs, and peopled with more and more independent "contractors", organized

---

[9] Kurt Vonnegut Jr. 1965. *Cat's Cradle.* New York: Dell, p. 187.

[10] Thomas W. Malone et al. 2003. *Inventing the Organizations of the 21st Century.* Cambridge, MA: The MIT Press.

as networks and associations, and having a key role in stewarding fluid project-based virtual organizations.

This vague prognostication is bound to leave everyone dissatisfied.

Indeed, it reveals the futility of trying to predict the future, for the future will be the result of "an outpouring of human creativity"[11] that will happen as a result of no grand plan and with no one in charge. Consequently, it is truly unpredictable.

Instead of predicting it, we have to work at creating it.

[11] Daniel Quinn. 1997. *My Ishmael.* New York: Bantam Books, p. 200-201.

Titles in the Collaborative Decentred Metagovernance Series

Other titles published by INVENIRE

12. Richard Clément et Caroline Andrew (sld)   2012
    Villes et langues : gouvernance et politiques
    Symposium international

11. Richard Clément and Caroline Andrew (eds)   2012
    Cities and Languages: Governance and Policy
    International Symposium

10. Michael Behiels and François Rocher (eds)   2011
    The State in Transition: Challenges for
    Canadian Federalism

9. Pierre Camu   2011
    La Flotte Blanche : Histoire de la Compagnie de
    Navigation du Richelieu et d'Ontario, 1845-1913

8. Rupak Chattopadhyay and Gilles Paquet (eds)   2011
    The Unimagined Canadian Capital:
    Challenges for the Federal Capital Region

7. Gilles Paquet   2011
    Tableau d'avancement II : Essais exploratoires sur la
    gouvernance d'un certain Canada français

6. James Bowen (ed)   2011
    The Entrepreneurial Effect: Waterloo

5. François Lapointe   2011
    Cities as Crucibles: Reflections on Canada's
    Urban Future

4. James Bowen (ed)   2009
    The Entrepreneurial Effect

3. Gilles Paquet   2009
    Scheming virtuously: the road to collaborative governance

2. Ruth Hubbard   2009
    Profession: Public Servant

1. Robin Higham   2009
    Who do we think we are: Canada's reasonable
    (and less reasonable) accommodation debates

www.ingramcontent.com/pod-product-compliance
Lightning Source LLC
Chambersburg PA
CBHW071601200326
41519CB00021BB/6830

9780776638829